FOOD LOVERS' SERIES

FOOD LOVERS
GUIDE TO
OKLAHOMA

The Best Restaurants, Markets & Local Culinary Offerings

1st Edition

Katie Johnstonbaugh

gpp

Guilford, Connecticut

Editor: Kevin Sirois
Project Editor: Lauren Brancato
Layout Artist: Mary Ballachino
Text Design: Sheryl Kober
Illustrations by Jill Butler with additional art by Carleen Moira Powell and MaryAnn Dubé
Maps: Melissa Baker © Morris Book Publishing, LLC

ISBN 978-0-7627-8115-7

Printed in the United States of America
10 9 8 7 6 5 4 3 2 1

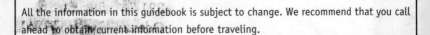

All the information in this guidebook is subject to change. We recommend that you call ahead to obtain current information before traveling.

Contents

Tulsa, 147

Recipes, 239

Appendices, 268

Index, 280

About the Author

Katie Johnstonbaugh remembers as a child being strangely unexcited by chain fast-food restaurants. While other kids were begging for pizza and bad burgers, she preferred to go to restaurants and order scalloped potatoes, ham and bean soup, and lobster. As she grew older, she realized she had a special passion for seeking out and finding food of noteworthy quality and has spent the past 3 years blogging about it on her blog, Dishin & Dishes (dishinanddishes.com). Here she shares everything from step-by-step recipes to restaurant gems the average person may not know about in Oklahoma and other places. By day she splits her time between working for the local school administration and doing a food segment featuring cooking and restaurants at KFOR-TV in Oklahoma City. She loves her evenings with her husband (whom she affectionately refers to as Mr. Wonderful) and their six kids and two dogs. Their family hub, the kitchen, is always a fun and eventful place for gatherings and new recipe creations.

Acknowledgments

First and foremost to my family—I have to thank my wonderful husband and best friend on the planet. Thanks to my Mr. Wonderful for putting up with a less-than-perfect house, as well as endless "date nights" with me venturing off to unheard-of places. To all my kids, Tori, Kayla, Conner, Chris, Jason, and Lyndsay, I love all of you very much. I know my time in writing has taken me away from you somewhat.

To my friends (Stephanie, Vivian, Joy and Dale, Nancy and Rick) who dined with me all over Oklahoma—it was culinary fun at its best with you!

To Globe Pequot Press—thank you for the wonderful opportunity, and many thanks to Kevin, my editor, for being patient with me.

To Rose and Genyce—you have been invaluable to me in helping me find sources of information for Tulsa and around the state I needed to complete this comprehensive guide.

To my readers in Oklahoma—you are why I love what I do. You guys are the best and it is still unbelievable to me that you read my garbled thoughts and obsessive food rants and raves!

To the chefs in Oklahoma . . . thank you for the hours you put in away from your families, the financial risks you've taken to start and run your businesses, and for the fabulous cuisine you give us!

Introduction

The official State Meal of Oklahoma might be what you expect—fried okra, squash, cornbread, barbecue pork, biscuits, sausage and gravy, grits, corn, strawberries, chicken-fried steak, black-eyed peas, and pecan pie. Though these things are well known and loved here, most have no idea of the vast cultural and culinary diversity that sweeps across our great plains (yes, along with the wind and tornadoes!). With our state ranking second in the production of natural gas and fifth in oil and wheat production, many foreign and out-of-state folk have been moving into Oklahoma for opportunity, and bringing with them a love of their own food cultures.

Oklahoma City has the largest number of eateries followed by Tulsa, but there are plenty of special places to eat elsewhere around our state, which have a grouping of their own following the Oklahoma City and Tulsa sections of the book. I encourage you to make the drive to one or more of these places as they are truly unique and loved by locals in and around the state!

How to Use This Book

Although this book covers Oklahoma as an entire state, I am focusing primarily on Oklahoma City, followed closely by Tulsa, and then some "can't-miss" restaurants around the state that we who live here love. Oklahoma City and Tulsa are broken down by popular neighborhoods or areas, and due to the great number of those, I've lumped several neighborhoods (designated in the chapter heading) together into a larger area.

Toward the back of the book, I hope you'll love and try to re-create some of the recipes from our beloved Oklahoma chefs. These will allow you to continue your Oklahoma visit through cooking its cuisine long after you leave our great state. If you are a current Oklahoma resident, I hope you'll journey away from your comfort zone a little and try out these local joints and fine-dining restaurants and not only support them but grow to love them as I do.

Foodie Faves

The restaurants that make up this section are the favorite restaurants that locals love to frequent often and that generate noteworthy buzz among foodies. These vary from long-standing places to new eateries that have generated noteworthy buzz with new and exciting or just plain wonderful cuisine among Oklahoman gastronomes.

Landmarks

These restaurants are those that have been around for a considerable amount of time and are known as dependable places to go for good cuisine. They are the "legends" of the Oklahoma food scene and can range from diners to fine dining.

Specialty Stores, Markets & Producers
Some truly fabulous specialized grocers, butcher shops, coffee shops, and bakeries that you won't want to miss in Oklahoma City and Tulsa.

Learn to Cook
Hone your cooking skills at these classrooms and establishments.

Recipes
Some of the state's best chefs have offered some of their own creations and widely loved recipes from their restaurants so that you can re-create them in your own home!

Price Code
The price code in this guide is based on the cost of one entree, excluding tax and tip.

$	less than $10
$$	$10 to $20
$$$	$20 to $30
$$$$	more than $30

Keeping Up with Food News

In Print

The *Oklahoman*, oklahoman.com. We are fortunate to have at our disposal the largest state newspaper in circulation in Oklahoma. Each Friday, the weekend food supplement features everything from new and old restaurants to recipes to all things culinary. MOOD is an online offspring of the *Oklahoman* and features various fun foodie facts and finds on their Cuisine page as well.

Tulsa World, tulsaworld.com. The *Tulsa World* covers food twice a week, the first being the food department of the Wednesday Scene section, with cooking and recipes by Nicole Marshall Middleton. Check it out for the latest happenings in the local food scene. Scott Cherry is the *World*'s restaurant critic and wine columnist. You can read his restaurant picks at tulsaworld.com/scene/food/restaurantguide/ or in the Weekend section in the print edition that comes out on Thursday.

The Oklahoma Gazette, okgazette.com. Stop off at any local joint and inside the door you're likely to see this paper magazine with all the latest on the local OKC scene. Included inside are restaurant features along with what's currently going on in Oklahoma City. You can also read current and back issues of the *Gazette* online for

The OK Food Dude

Dave Cathey, aka The Food Dude, is affectionately called "The Godfather" by the other Oklahoma City food writers, and for good reason. Dave is always on top of the latest in Oklahoma cuisine and blogs about it on his *Oklahoman* Food Editor blog (blog .newsok.com/fooddude). From restaurant openings and closings to how to do a "Bone Marrow Luge," you'll want to check him out for the latest on the gastronomic scene. He also dishes out some fabulous recipes!

free at okgazette.com—click on the Restaurants tab for fabulous restaurant listings, restaurant reviews, food and drink features, and Bite Size, a bite-size portion of what's happening during the week in Oklahoma City.

Urban Tulsa Weekly, urbantulsaweekly.com. The *Urban Tulsa Weekly* is an independent weekly newspaper distributed to the Tulsa metropolitan area each Thursday and can also be read online. Their Cuisine Scene section has great restaurant listings and also features restaurant reviews and articles. Reading it online gives viewers a selection of drop-downs to pick breakfast/lunch/dinner choices.

Tulsa People, tulsapeople.com. This award-winning magazine comes out once a month and is great at showcasing Tulsa places and the people who make them happen. Their Dining section features all things gastronomic, from wine talk to restaurants to food events happening around the Tulsa area. They have fabulous photography as well.

Oklahoma Bloggers

TravelOK.com. A bevy of information about Oklahoma, including things to do, with breakdowns by City, Hotels and Lodging, and Festivals and Events. Check out their Dining section and search by cuisine, city, and other search tools offered.

EataroundOKC.com. The writers for this site have truly eaten their way around Oklahoma City and have the greatest variety of reviewed restaurants in the Oklahoma City area. Their website gives pricing information and has photo links to their Facebook page showing the food they eat.

Stephaniebice.com. This newcomer is passionate about restaurants in Oklahoma City and just began writing reviews in 2012, but she knows her stuff and offers great food recommendations. I also enjoy hanging out with her while we eat at a new place. She is a kindred foodie spirit.

Tulsafood.com. Founded by Brian McCullough and expanded now to several food contributors, this site is incredibly informative for the Tulsa area. Broken down by areas and/or cuisine, there is almost no restaurant they haven't visited.

The Pioneer Woman, thepioneerwoman.com. If you haven't heard of Ree Drummond by now, you've been living under a rock. This rancher's wife turned food blogger now has her own Food Network show, a best-selling cookbook, and posts recipes several times a week while wading through cow dung as well.

Joe's Burger Search, joesburgersearch.com. Joe has one culinary mission and that is to search around (mostly the Tulsa area, but really any burger is subject to his scrutiny) and report back to you the reader about every last place on earth that serves a burger within his reach. Sort of like a burger documentary, and Joe knows burgers, plain and simple.

The Tulsa Food Guy, tulsafoodguy.com. Dedicated to eating "all things manly," Tulsa Food Guy explores burgers, BBQ, steak, sausage and all other types of man food in the Tulsa area. It has an interesting cast of characters, from the Duke of Earlsboro (Oklahoma) to his grandpa "Papa Ray" and it's always entertaining.

Taste Oklahoma, tasteoklahoma.com. This husband-and-wife team works in the tourism industry and loves to write about anything to do with Oklahoma, including dining, wine, and even Korean food.

Tasha Does Tulsa, tashadoestulsa.com. The purpose of Natasha Ball's blog is to let Tulsa folk know they don't need to be bored, and much of her content includes restaurant reviews. I love her fun sense of humor and interesting facts about things in Tulsa.

Food Events

January

Chocolate Festival, Norman, OK; normanchocolatefestival.com. The Chocolate Festival in Norman, ranked third by the Food Network under Best Food Festivals and featured in *Southern Living* magazine, is every chocolate lover's dream. A fund-raiser for the Norman Firehouse Art Center, the Chocolate Festival features chocolate confections by 40 chocolate vendors. Participants get a cake-size lidded box to fill up with the sweet treats that range from the famed chocolate mice from La Baguette to silky smooth hot chocolate.

February

Frederick Fantastic Oyster Fry, Frederick's Prather Brown Center, 211 S. 13th St., Frederick, OK; frederickokchamber.org/oysterfry. A tradition since 1952, when Bramlett Johnson decided to bring back oysters from the Gulf of Mexico to share with his friends and family, this festival has escalated into quite a party!

Enjoy raw and fried oysters along with a bevy of side dishes like coleslaw, chips, and bread. On top of this, raw oysters can be purchased by the gallon as long as quantities last. There is also an arts and crafts show of local artists

German Feast and Auction, Corn Bible Academy, 208 N. Reimer St., Corn, OK; cornbible.com. The authentic German food served at this event includes *verenika,* a German pastry specialty of dough wrapped around an egg and cottage cheese mixture; cracklins made in a 40-gallon cauldron; and smoked sausage, sauerkraut, and desserts patterned after food the Mennonite settlers of the area would have enjoyed in the early 1900s. There is also a silent auction at this festival and sale in the auditorium. Also available at the festival is a cookbook full of authentic German recipes.

March

Chef's Feast, Oklahoma City, OK; regionalfoodbank.org. The best and the brightest of 25 top restaurants and chefs come together to provide internationally themed cuisine, a wine pull, and more. If you get a chance to go to this food and wine tasting event, you'll be glad you did, and all donations go to the Regional Food Bank's Food for Kids programs. This is a fun-filled event and always looked forward to by all Oklahoma City foodies each year.

April

Festival of the Arts, Oklahoma City, OK; artscouncilokc.com/ festival-of-the-arts. This festival has been held downtown since 1967 and always breaks us Oklahomans out of spring fever! It is held in downtown Oklahoma City at the Festival Plaza and the Myriad Botanical Gardens. It runs from 11 a.m. to 9 p.m. and has free admission. Visual, performing, and culinary arts are all offered up to festival goers in this large forum in downtown Oklahoma City. Many local restaurants have booths at this event on International Food Row. Even if you're not an art fan, the food is worth going for.

Muskogee Chili & BBQ Cook-Off, Civic Center Market Square Festival Area, 5th and Boston Streets, Muskogee, OK; exchangeclubmuskogee.org/chilicookoff. Enjoy a full day of entertainment, drinks, chili, and BBQ for the entire family! There is a kids' zone with inflatables for your family enjoyment, and pony and camel rides as well. Attendees can purchase a taster kit and sample chili, barbecued chicken, and pork. This one lasts all day! There is plenty of live music to keep your feet moving as well as the Azalea Festival Parade.

Roberts Ranch Smokin' Red Dirt BBQ & Music Festival, Enid, OK; reddirtbbq.com. This event is a sanctioned Kansas

Oklahoma Weather

Weather in Oklahoma can range from the really crazy (in the panhandle towns like Guymon) to the beautiful at any given time. You might find yourself playing flag football at Thanksgiving in shorts or bundling up in a parka depending on what the weather gods of the month dole out. Oklahoma is in a unique weather belt of sorts where the cold air from the north, the warm air of the south and the jetstream unite within its borders, so you could encounter just about anything. Those from the north will be happy to visit in the winter, when we might have weather in the 70s and 80s. Those who love heat will want to visit in the summer when we're pushing 90s, but I truly love the spring and the fall, where you'll see sunny days and gorgeous blooms or foliage. Stroll through some of our Oklahoma City walking districts, like Paseo Arts District or Western Avenue, and experience lovely weather when the northern states are knee-deep in snow.

City Barbecue Society state competition. People's Choice picks the winner and lucky attendees get to sample the rib offerings. There is a "make and take" craft fair that is free for children from kindergarten through 5th grade, an evening of local talent at the Gaslight Theatre and in the evening free pulled-pork sandwiches. For a small price visitors can also sample the offerings of more than 20 participating contestants. Also at night is a fireworks display!

May

Bixby BBQ-n-Music Festival, 137th Street and S. Memorial Drive, Bixby, OK; bixbyrotarybbq.com. Be adventurous at this festival and buy a $10 "taster kit" and sample every competitor's offerings while listening to over 10 different blues and jazz musicians play throughout the two day event. There is also a kids' zone, a tractor train ride, carnival games, and plenty of beer to go around.

El Reno Fried Onion Burger Day Festival, El Reno, OK; elrenoburgerday.wordpress.com. Held as a tribute to the fried onion burger El Reno helped to make famous, this event centers around one thing: the world's largest onion burger being grilled in the center of town. Festival goers get a chunk of it and there are also live music, car shows, game booths, arts and crafts, and rides.

National Indian Taco Championship, Pawhuska, OK; osagetribe .com. If you haven't experienced an Indian taco, this is a must-attend Oklahoma food event. There are also live bands and dancing. Anyone can be a judge by purchasing a ticket and helping taste these puffy fried-dough tacos that are truly unique.

Prague Kolache Festival, Prague, OK; praguekolachefestival .com. Held each first Saturday in May, this Czech festival features dance, song, food, and crafts along with music and street dancing in the evening. And of course, there are *kolaches,* a wonderful pastry that may hold everything from dollops of fruit to the stuffed variety that contains a savory treat like meat or cheese inside of its pillow of baked dough. People from around the world come to this event. There is an entertainment grandstand with Czech music playing all day and a carnival with plenty of food booths. Stay for the parade and into the night for the concerts and street dancing, especially the Chicken Dance, which also brings lots of laughter.

Stillwell Strawberry Festival, Stillwell, OK; strawberrycapital.com. This festival has been going strong since 1948 and is highly anticipated each year. The free ice cream and strawberries draw tens of thousands a year to this festival but there 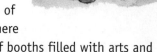 are also a 5K run, a rodeo, and plenty of booths filled with arts and fair food as well!

Tabouleh Fest, Bristow, OK; visitbristowok.com/special/ taboulehfest.htm. Tabouleh is obviously the star of this festival, which celebrates the Lebanese heritage of Bristow with traditional belly dancers, food, music, and carnival rides. There is a tabouleh recipe contest as well as something else that's fun—visitors will want to make sure they don't miss the tabouleh bar, where they can mix up their own variety of tabouleh.

June

Battle of the Burger, Norman, OK; battleoftheburger.com. A panel of local celebrities and officials judge this competition to see who makes the best burger in Central Oklahoma. Enter the contest if you think you have a great recipe or just show up for samples! Also enjoy live music, children's activities and a silent auction.

Stratford Peach Festival, Stratford City Park, Stratford, OK; stratfordok.org. Stratford is known as the peach capital of the state and each year at this festival fun is everywhere to be seen. This weekend event has three star attractions: a free pancake breakfast in the morning, located in the FFA barn; the mid-morning peach cook-off; and the car show all day. There is also a parade, concerts, and plenty of food featuring the star . . . peaches, of course! The homemade peach ice cream is to die for.

August

Oklahoma Championship Cook-Off-Tulsa, 6th Street and Detroit Avenue and 6th Street and Boston Avenue, Tulsa, OK; oksteakcookoff.com. Things sizzle in downtown Tulsa, where teams compete to see who can make the best steak. Before the event there is appetizer sampling and for a $20 ticket, attendees get a 16-ounce steak and fixings. There is also a beer garden located near the main stage.

Rush Springs Watermelon Festival, Rush Springs, OK; mac-vincent.com/Festival.htm. Want to try your hand (I mean mouth) at a seed-spitting contest? If not, there is a bevy of fun family activities at this very popular long-standing festival. Oh, and there's plenty of free watermelon to go around! Over 50,000 pounds of watermelons are served each year to festival visitors.

World's Largest Calf Fry Festival & Cook Off, Vinita, OK; vinita.com/calf_fry. It's not nicknamed the "testicle festival" for nothing. Keep an open mind and try these local "delicacies" that most people actually think are delicious. This festival offers up over 2,000 pounds of calf fries each year. If that's not your thing, there is plenty of other cowboy food to go and also some cowboy games as well. For the kids there are crafts, games, a baseball tournament, and large inflatables. Check out the Will Rogers Memorial Rodeo toward the end of the event!

September

Oklahoma State Fair, Oklahoma Fairgrounds, 333 Gordon Cooper Blvd., Oklahoma City, OK; (405) 948-6704; okstatefair.com. Disney on Ice, the circus, the rodeo, five exhibit halls, countless musical offerings, and livestock and horse shows all are featured at this fair that brings in over a million folks each year. But the food is the real draw here, and the bites on offer include cinnamon rolls, chocolate bacon, roasted fresh corn, Indian tacos, funnel cakes, and turkey legs.

Oklahoma State Sugar Arts Show, Tulsa, OK; oklahomasugar artists.com. Sometimes the quality of one sugared rose petal can make all the difference. Featured on the Food Network, this competition allows you to watch some of the nation's best pastry chefs from around the world create wedding cake works of art in the bustling atmosphere of the Tulsa State Fair.

October

Blue Bell's Taste of Summer, 8201 E. Hwy. 51, Broken Arrow, OK; (918) 258-5100; bluebell.com. Blue Bell Creameries is one of the pride and joys of Oklahoma. Their milk and other dairy offerings have satisfied us for years, especially the ice cream. At this festival you can take your family on a self-guided tour through the Blue Bell Creameries, listen to live music, let your kids do the Jupiter Jump, and join in an ice cream eating contest. Oh, and did I mention the all-you-can-eat ice cream?

Slow Food Picnic, Oklahoma City, OK; slowfoodokc.com. Held outdoors, this picnic is a quaint family fun time of sack races, pony rides, music, and games. The local food of Oklahoma is the star feature and is celebrated all evening. Visitors will experience the pleasure of local chefs cooking local harvest, meat, and dairy products in a feast that will delight everyone and is served home-style to each picnic table. An additional supplement to your ticket price gets you all the local beer and wine you can drink.

Tulsa Oktoberfest, Tulsa, OK; tulsaoktoberfest.org. This Oktoberfest boasts a carnival by the riverside, imported German beer, and tons of fun events like polka and chicken dancing. But it's the food that will keep you there, like schnitzel sandwiches, Bavarian cheesecake, German potato salad, bratwurst with sauerkraut, knackwurst and polish sausages, potato pancakes, and fresh apple strudel. Tulsa claims that the Chicken Dance originated at their Oktoberfest so you must do it while you're there.

Watonga Cheese Festival, Watonga, OK; watongacheesefestival .com. A cheese food contest that hosts six divisions all based on cheese, from main dishes to vegetables, is the key at this festival. There are also cheese tastings that will leave you happy, along with many food vendors, a parade, a car show, a quilt show, an art show, and many other features including a Rat Race, a fun one-mile run that anyone can enter.

December

Minco Honey Festival, Minco, OK; minco-ok.com/ minco/festival.htm The Minco Honey Festival began over 20 years ago and has grown into quite an event. Get a tour of the Ross Honey Plant with owners Jim and Glenda Ross, take a sample of the honey bake-off and sample honey, cheese, and milk products from local producers. There is a kiddie tractor pull on tiny tractors, a pancake breakfast, and Santa Claus is downtown as well. The Antique Road Show lets participants learn about their home treasures and there is a local tour of homes. It is set close to Christmas so you can enjoy the seasonal decor and enjoy the delicious food all at once! Check the website for the location of the various events.

Food Trucks

The food truck scene in Oklahoma has been around for a while but mainly in the taqueria/taco truck sense. On the weekend, if you drive down SW 29th Street, Oklahoma City, you will see a variety of taco trucks in a variety of parking lots. There are a few other notable trucks that have cropped up in the metro area or have been around forever that I will mention. As they are mobile food trucks and subject to be just about anywhere, I've included Twitter handles and Facebook pages where applicable. This is about the best way to stay updated daily on where they may be at any given time. We here in Oklahoma look forward to this new era of foodie heaven coming our way as new trucks open in the future.

Al's Food Truck & Mobile Catering, 705 S. Mustang Rd., Yukon, OK 73099; wildals.webs.com; @WildAls; facebook.com/pages/Wild-Als-Food-Truck-Mobile-Catering. Al is wild, that's for sure. He's wild about cooking up some wicked good fare on his truck. After being in the food industry for 15 years, Al decided to venture out on his own and cook food the way he likes it. And we, the fortunate folk in Oklahoma City, are glad that he did. Visit this truck out and about or at events and sample some delicious dishes like pimiento cheese brisket burgers or pork stir-fry wraps. Al also makes his own rubs and sauces and they are fantastic on any of his sandwiches. Check out his Facebook page for daily offerings.

Big Truck Tacos, Oklahoma City, OK; @bigtrucktacos. While they also have a stationary store, owner Chris Lower and chefs Cally Johnson and Kathryn Mathis are the creative minds behind Big Truck Tacos. The truck is mobile all day long and announces its location on Twitter or Facebook. Gourmet tacos are served up like the Flaming Lips (named after a local rocker), which is actually made of hickory-smoked tongue—not lips—pico de gallo, sliced avocado, and *queso fresco*. Big Truck won the coveted cash prize after season one of *The Great Food Truck Race* on the Food Network, when they received the most votes in the country from die-hard local fans.

Bobo's Chicken, 1812 NE 23rd St., Oklahoma City, OK 73111. Look for the bright red food trailer and, obviously, plan on taking your order to go. I promise you, it's worth it. Touted by foodies as the best fried (and smoked) chicken in Oklahoma, this Oklahoma City legend is only open on Friday and Saturday nights, usually after 6 p.m. (they stay open until 2 or 3 a.m.). You pick the number of chicken pieces and they are served with fries and fry bread and all is drizzled nicely with honey. Try the catfish or shrimp if you prefer, but chicken is their specialty and the local favorite.

Cupcakes to Go, Oklahoma City, OK; (405) 330-2190; cupcakes2gogo .com; @cupcakestogogo; facebook.com/cupcakestogogo. Melany Boughman created Cupcakes to Go to be a vacation of sorts, traveling through culinary destinations with family desserts, childhood favorites, and made-from-scratch daily creations of moist cake, creamy icing, and a variety of toppings to satisfy your sweets cravings. She also caters events, so check out her site for delicious cupcake flavors like Japanese Chocolate Cherry Blossoms

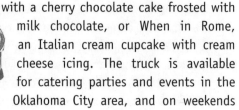

with a cherry chocolate cake frosted with milk chocolate, or When in Rome, an Italian cream cupcake with cream cheese icing. The truck is available for catering parties and events in the Oklahoma City area, and on weekends can be found near the downtown library around the general vicinity of Hudson and Park Avenue.

Hot Dog Locos, Martinez Tires parking lot on SW 29th Street, Oklahoma City, OK 73119. Noel and Sandra Valdez grill up some amazing hotdogs on their truck and they make them one way. They use all-beef dogs, flat griddle them with thick slices of bacon wrapped in a spiral around them, and then they top them with sweet grilled onions, sliced avocados and an amazing tomatillo- and habañero-based "green sauce" that will make you want to go searching them out time and time again. Each dog comes with fried pork rinds and your choice of drink.

Hot Dog OKC, Oklahoma City, OK; hotdogokc.com; @HotDogOKC. From her hilarious tweets to her hot dogs named after local celebrities, Gale VanCampen and her wiener cart are always in two or three locations downtown on the weekend. She serves up delicious Nathan's hotdogs and is prone to name them after local news personalities. For instance, there is the Joleen Chaney dog named for the KFOR anchor/reporter, and topped with mustard and lots of jalapeños for a spicy kick, or the Emily Sutton and the 4 Warned Frank (named after the KFOR weather gal), which is topped with a mustard "tornado" and a "debris" of onions. You can find out on Twitter where and what she'll be serving up daily as well. Her personality is unfailingly fun and her dogs aren't bad either!

Tacos Los Compadres, Bill's Used Furniture parking lot, 1118 N. Berry Rd., Norman, OK 73069; (405) 329-7400. The big white truck sporting the TLC logo (Tacos Los Compadres) is parked in the Bill's Used Furniture parking lot at Alameda and Porter and has some of the best tacos and *tortas* around. As with any food truck, you'll take your order to go and seating is available at the picnic table next to the truck that has a large tented awning over it. The tacos are plentiful and delicious and come wrapped in foil with some lime wedges and a good helping of your choice of meat. But you must try the *tortas,* which are grilled on the truck's homemade bread and stuffed full of all kinds of wonderful stuff.

Taqueria Sanchez, Around the 4000-5000 block of NW 10th Street, Oklahoma City, OK. This white truck with red letters offers some deliciously pleasing authentic Mexican street tacos, burritos, *tortas,* and gorditas in choices like *al pastor,* chicken, *asada, lengua,* and *barbacoa.* The burritos are more than enough for one person and the *asada* quesadilla is delicious, and the great news is . . . all the tacos are only one dollar! Grab a cold Jarritos to wash it all down.

Waffle Champion, Oklahoma City, OK; (405) 525-9235; @ wafflechampion; facebook.com/wafflechampion. Tara Taylor and Waffle Champion president Todd Woodruff serve up waffles with or without chicken. There are sweet and savory waffles and each is wrapped around its fillings like a soft taco. The menu is written on the chalkboard by the truck and you might see things like a breakfast waffle of thick-cut bacon, gourmet cheddar, and farm eggs. You might also see a lunch taco of pulled pork, brown rice, a fried farm egg, and cracklins. This truck is building a huge following for how new it is, and I think it will only get bigger! Waffle Champion has plans to open a storefront operation at the 1212 Building in Midtown and diners can expect to see it open in the spring of 2013. For now, look for the truck mostly on the corner of NW 23rd Street and Walker.

Oklahoma City

Oklahoma City

Oklahoma City has a wonderfully diverse choice of cuisine, perhaps not expected in the heart of the Southwest. From the Asian District and large Vietnamese population (called Little Saigon) in Oklahoma City to the Italian lovers in Krebs to the Korean population in Midwest City, plus our large Latin and Hispanic community that has worked its way upward from nearby Mexico, you will find a bevy of restaurants, markets, and specialty shops for just about every culture. Oklahoma City has one of the largest actual land masses of any city in the United States, and for that reason there are many different districts across the region with differing clusters and areas of eateries.

Oklahoma City is evolving into a place to visit and have a ball, from our MAPS plan that is renovating downtown and Bricktown into a happening place, to strolling down the mile-long Bricktown Canal, catching an Oklahoma City Thunder basketball game, or cruising on the Bricktown Water Taxis on the Canal. You can visit the Oklahoma River and rent a kayak, stand-up paddle board, or bicycle from March through October or visit Stockyards City and watch real cowboys at work and shop the Western shops. There is also a huge project being planned called Core to Shore, from central downtown to the river, that will be building Central Park, with a pedestrian trail, a "Great Lawn" for events and concerts that will accommodate 20,000 event goers, a children's area with a jump-right-in fountain water park, shopping, offices, and maybe even a giant Ferris wheel.

Oklahoma City Central

Asian, Belle Isle, Paseo Arts & Western Avenue Districts

This grouping in Oklahoma City includes many up and coming developments, some of them old historic districts that are being revived and some that are just coming alive. A big part of these artsy neighborhoods is the food scene that is growing within them. They are somewhat off the beaten path of main thoroughfares of the greater Oklahoma City area, but like any treasure, they are worth seeking out and exploring.

The Asian-American population of Oklahoma City is the highest in the state and lies in the central part of the city. Little Saigon, as it's also called, began in the '70s when scads of Vietnamese refugees headed to Oklahoma City after the fall of Saigon. Why Oklahoma you might ask? A small group of activists rescued the refugees from the camp in Fort Chaffee, Arkansas, just across the state line and brought them to Oklahoma City. They settled here to become masonry workers, builders, and warehouse workers and in time educated themselves to become so much more. Businesses, including restaurants, began to pop up, among them many Vietnamese, Chinese, and Thai restaurants. Drive through our Asian District on any given day and you will be overwhelmed with the many *pho* eateries you will pass.

The Belle Isle District is one of the most exciting new expansions for food lovers in northwest Oklahoma City right now. Located between Classen and Western, the addition of the Classen Curve development includes numerous wonderful local eateries and a brand-new Whole Foods store. Also included in Belle Isle is a generous stretch of restaurants near Penn Square mall along the Northwest Expressway, one of our main corridors.

Stretching between 28th and North Walker to 30th and Dewey, Paseo is the oldest arts district in Oklahoma City. With more than 17 galleries and 60 artists, it is only natural that creative food should be present here as well. During the First Friday Gallery Walk that occurs each month, many eateries offer specials. Friday night you'll enjoy many art openings, wine tastings, and live music. On Saturday you can see artists at work giving live demonstrations.

Western Avenue is another very artsy district consisting of antiques shops, art galleries, corporate offices, quaint boutiques, and of course, restaurants. Wednesdays on Western happen each week and offer patrons special discounts and savings. You can visit the website to learn more at visitwesternavenue.com. Many fabulous eateries are located on or near Western Avenue.

Belle Isle Restaurant & Brewing Company, 1900 NW Expy., Belle Isle District, Oklahoma City, OK 73118; (405) 840-1911; belleislerestaurant.com; Brewpub; $$. This brewpub is located in the swank 50 Penn Places in northwest Oklahoma City. They keep their kitchen open late with a late-night menu featuring items like beer-battered mushrooms, fish-and-chips, or fish tacos. They also have a full bar including handcrafted beers like their Power House Porter, a full-bodied dark beer with a roasted finish, or their popular oatmeal stout. Sipping on all this beer is going to make you want to snack on something delicious, so don't overlook the pizzas on the menu either. The Okie Pork Pie has slow-roasted pulled pork, honey-pepper bacon, mozzarella cheese, and red sauce, and on Monday, you get them for a steal with the $5.95 special! They also have nightly offerings of bingo, trivia, sports nights, and they feature live music on the weekend, so don't forget to check the website for the band schedule.

Cafe Antigua, 1903 N. Classen Blvd., Asian District, Oklahoma City, OK 73106; (405) 602-8984; Latin American; $. You might spot Cafe Antigua and think nothing of it while driving by, but if you do drive by, you'll miss out on some terrific Latin American cuisine. While it's nothing fancy to look at inside, they serve up some delectable goodies, especially their breakfast dishes. Try the Motuleno Double Stack and ask them to add chorizo. You'll swoon over three corn tortillas with black beans and three eggs that are topped with avocado, *queso fresco, queso seco,* parsley and a lovely pinkish-red tomato sauce called *chirmol.* Also for lunch, try the *chuletas mayas,* which I adore. This scrumptious dish is a slightly spicy mix of black beans and rice topped with onion, tomato, cilantro, parsley, and topped with two lovely spiced pork chops. Make sure you use the spicy green sauce that accompanies pretty much everything. Wash everything down with some cool mango juice and for dessert try their Fried Plantains in Glory, which are plantains fried in brown sugar, cinnamon, and Kahlua and topped with a dollop of sour cream. This goes wonderfully with their authentic Guatemalan coffee.

Cafe Nova, 4308 N. Western Ave, Western Avenue District, Oklahoma City, OK 73118; (405) 525-6682; Cafe; $$$. Entering Cafe Nova for the first time, you'll love the retro funky feel of the main room. A giant, softly lit, curved white bar arches around the entire front of the restaurant; local artists' paintings hang on

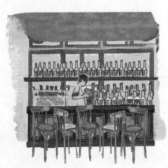

the brick walls; and black tablecloths make you feel like you're eating inside an urban artist's studio. The bar is a popular hangout for yuppies and artsy folk alike where you can sit and snack on their Gourmet Tots, complete with Parmesan, cheddar, and ham and a dipping sauce of homemade ranch dressing while drinking local or imported beer or wine. Their blackened ahi tuna is

Home-Grown Chains:
Johnnie's Charcoal Broiler

The first Johnnie's (johnniesburgers.com) opened in 1971 and was a 12 car-hop stall with a very small indoor dining area. People loved it and thus began Johnnie's expansion. The full restaurant was finally opened in 1981 and since then other locations have been cropping up all over the state bringing their total to eight restaurants. David and Rick Haynes still run this long-standing chain and are proud of the fact that they use a personal touch on everything they make, including grilling their burgers over charcoal. At Johnnie's, you get some fabulous burgers, fries and their famous onion rings, which are sliced fresh daily and hand battered. The burgers are served without a lot of fuss but with good down home ingredients like their house-made hickory sauce. At their Britton Road location, you can also get some wonderful homemade gelato at their adjacent gelato bar, Giovanni's. Johnnie's has four full-service locations (burgers, fries, salads, sandwiches) and three express (breakfast and burgers only) locations.

cooked perfectly (rare) and melts in your mouth and the On Western Meatloaf is enough to feed two.

Cafe 501, 5825 NW Grand Blvd., Belle Isle District, Oklahoma City, OK 73118; (405) 844-1501; Steaks/Seafood; $$. One would never know Cafe 501 started out 15 years ago as a humble cafe. The decor is very New York swank, airy and modern. If it's nice outside, sit out on benches by their retro fountains and chat with a friend while you wait for a table. For starters, the ahi tuna tartare is wonderful and comes mixed up with avocado, cucumber relish, sriracha soy, and drizzled with a wasabi crème fraîche and served in a rice paper crisp. Also try their slow-roasted sirloin, which is not your ordinary roast. It's slow-cooked and covered in a Cabernet demi-glace. Saturday morning you must try their french toast, made with homemade brioche bread, or drop in for Sunday brunch. Don't leave without trying one of the wonderful baked goods like a red velvet brownie or German chocolate cookie. An additional location is at 501 S. Boulevard St., Edmond, OK 73034; (405) 551-8038.

Cheever's Cafe, 2409 N. Hudson Ave., Paseo Arts District, Oklahoma City, OK 73103; (405) 525-7007; cheeverscafe.com; Brunch/Cafe Fare/Southwestern; $$$. What once held a legendary flower shop near the Paseo District is now a gem to behold in the dining scene. Nestled in the historic district, this place is quaint, trendy, and deliciously Southwest. Executive Chef Mark Ridener delivers sophisticated Southwest flavors at their finest. Start out dinner with roasted chicken and pepper jack strudel with layers of roasted chicken, green chiles and pepper jack cheese stuffed between phyllo dough. Cheever's also has a superb Sunday brunch with my favorite, *masa vallo con huevos,* shrimp risotto topped with two masa cakes, poached eggs, *pico* and *ancho* cream and served with a wonderful salsa verde. Have a Bloody Mary made with jalapeño juice or a mimosa and end the meal by cooling down your palate with the giant "Grand Canyon" carrot cake. Sure, you can split it, but after one bite you just may keep it all for yourself.

Chow's Chinese, 3033 N. May Ave., Asian District, Oklahoma City, OK 73107; (405) 949-1663; Chinese; $$. While the decor at Chow's may not be fine dining, the food most certainly is. Owner and namesake Max Chow hails from Hong Kong and is very picky about the freshness and authenticity of all of his ingredients. Start out with my favorite: the five-spice fried quail or try the crispy tofu with scallions and garlic. Feast on roasted duck that will make your eyes roll backward or try the lobster or oysters, which are flown in fresh each Thursday. Of notable mention are any of the panfried noodle dishes. The crispy noodles soak in the delectable sauces and become a thing of greatness. Ask the chef to prepare any one of their fish dishes like the sea bass with cilantro and you won't be sorry.

Classen Grill, 5122 Classen Circle, Belle Isle District, Oklahoma City, OK 73118; (405) 842-0428; Cafe; $. One of the staple places in Oklahoma City to go for a great breakfast, Classen Grill combines a diner with a gourmet food experience, with wonderful things like fresh squeezed orange juice and *migas,* a Southwest breakfast with tortilla strips fried then mixed in with eggs and meat. For you Elvis fans, there is a Memphis french toast complete with bread stuffed with peanut butter, bananas, and honey, then dipped in cinnamon batter and grilled. For another Southwest treat, try the three-layer enchilada with its stacked corn tortilla layers filled with chicken, scrambled eggs, cheese, sour cream sauce, black olives, and more. Try one of their burgers for lunch and you'll see that Classen Grill isn't just about their delicious breakfasts.

Deep Fork Grill, 5418 N. Western Ave, Western Avenue District, Oklahoma City, OK 73118; (405) 848-7678; deepforkgrill.com; Steak House/Seafood; $$$. Whether you're looking for an intimate booth for two, or a socially fun-filled evening, Deep Fork Grill fits the bill for both needs. Under the tutelage of Chef Victor Izeta, Deep Fork is a favorite among local diners and has been for years. Try their most loved appetizer, the chicken brochette: tender bites of chicken wrapped around artichoke hearts and then in bacon and covered with a chipotle aioli that makes your taste buds scream for joy. Deep Fork features an extensive organic, sustainably produced, and biodynamic wine list, and I suggest sampling a glass while nibbling on their fruit and cheese platter. The standout main course is the braised beef short ribs that are fall-off-the-bone tender and covered in a sweet and spicy chipotle-molasses glaze. Deep Fork has something for everyone, including wood-fired pizzas and even vegetarian offerings. My very personal favorite at Deep Fork is their delectable mac and cheese, which is a blend of truffled Asiago cream, smoked tomatoes, and softened leeks capped off with a smattering of crunchy bread crumbs.

Fung's Kitchen, 3231 N. Classen Blvd., Asian District, Oklahoma City, OK 73118; (405) 524-4133; Chinese; $$. Fung's Kitchen is not your typical Chinese-American restaurant. The chef hails from Hong Kong and offers up true Cantonese cuisine. Known for their roasted duck hanging in the glass display that you can purchase by the quarter, half, or whole, Fung's also goes heavy on seafood. Order off the Cantonese menu instead of the American version, and get wonderful dishes like braised duck with assorted meats or the King's Special panfried noodles. Delight in the Peking spareribs with their spectacular Asian glaze and health it up with an order of snow tip peas. Try one of their wonderful clay hot pots like the chicken thigh pot stir fried and served in a special sauce. Go with a group and sit at the lazy Susan table so you can share several dishes at once and experience this truly unique dining experience.

Inca Trail Peruvian Restaurant, 10948-A N. May Ave., NW Oklahoma City, Oklahoma City, OK 73120; (918) 286-0407; incatrailokc.com; Peruvian; $$. Peruvian food is on the rise in Oklahoma City, due to the Latin markets now importing all the delicious native peppers like the *amarillo, panca,* and *rocoto.* Chef Niel Zambrano dishes up some delicious fare at Inca Trail Peruvian Restaurant by using old family recipes and Spanish, African, and Asian influences in every bite. Start off with the amazing *papa a la huancaina,* a delicious Peruvian potato salad of sorts covered in the yellow sauce made of the *aji amarillo* blended with milk and cheeses. Perhaps one of the most beloved Peruvian main dishes is *lomo saltado* with beef or chicken, which is a flavor explosion for your taste buds. If you are a ceviche fan, no one does it better than Inca Trail and there are many choices to pick from. For a refreshing drink, try a *chicha morada,* a semisweet Peruvian drink made of purple corn, pineapple, spices, and sugar.

Lee's Sandwiches, 3300 N. Classen Blvd., Asian District, Oklahoma City, OK 73118 (405) 601-2161; leesandwiches.com; Vietnamese; $. The line at Lee's is always full of eager bustling business folks looking to get their hands on some delicious *banh mi* sandwiches. Lee's has quite the selection of toppings from the classic pork and pâté to the *jambon* and pork roll. All come on fresh-baked crusty French baguettes and are topped with julienned pickled daikon radishes and carrots, a sprig of cilantro and some jalapeño pepper slices. Grab a French loaf to go for one buck before you leave. Need something fresh to drink? Try a fresh-squeezed juice like their carrot drink or honeydew drink or try one of their iced taro beverages. Lee's also has numerous offerings of baked goods like giant muffins and chocolate croissants or *pâté chaud* (a meat-filled pastry). And for dessert, try one of the unique flavors of ice cream like Awesome Avocado, Jiving Jackfruit, taro, or lychee. Or, if you're there at 11 a.m. the cream cake machine will be pumping out custard-filled little treats, so pick up a box and take it with you.

The Lobby Cafe & Bar, 4322 N. Western Ave., Western Avenue District, Oklahoma City, OK 73118; (405) 604-4650; Cafe; $$.

From Chef Mackenzie Bentley's delectable offerings of tapas using as much local produce as she can find, and located adjacent to the world-renowned Will Rogers Theatre, The Lobby Bar has some of the best food and atmosphere around. Legendary Chef Kurt Fleischfresser and owner Carl Milam have a place in Lobby Cafe & Bar that other chefs say they'd like to lunch at. The Lobby offers unique sliders, including their lobster slider complete with saffron aioli and shrimp or a No Name Ranch short rib slider, named after the local ranch that supplies the beef and topped off with horseradish mayo. The Lobby Bar also serves up some fantastic sandwiches and is a late-night favorite for mixologist creations of many happening folk in Oklahoma City. Try their fabulous specialty coffees and breakfast as well.

Matthew Kenney OKC, 5820 N. Classen Blvd., Ste. 1, Belle Isle District, Oklahoma City, OK 73118; (405) 842-1050; matthewkenneycuisine.com/restaurants; Raw Food/Vegan; $$. Voted one of America's Best New Restaurants by *Forbes* magazine in 2011, raw-food chef Matthew Kenney's place has altered the gastronomic landscape of Oklahoma with a classy and organic upscale raw-food restaurant and academy. The menu changes in spring and fall, but try one of the long-standing appetizers on the menu like the Avocado Dragon Roll, a lovely sushi roll filled with vegetables and chopped jicama instead of rice. Or try a staple from the main menu: the Classic Heirloom Lasagna stacked with layers of sun-cured marinara, macadamia ricotta, and hand-cut pesto and capped off with a beautifully ripened heirloom tomato. Don't leave

CHEF SPOTLIGHT: MATTHEW KENNEY

Matthew Kenney was once thought of as the newest rising star in New York City. He arrived there in 1993 and opened Matthew's on the Upper East Side. The following year Matthew was named one of *Food & Wine*'s 10 Best New Chefs in America and nominated as a Rising Star Chef by the James Beard Foundation. He then opened Bar Anise, Mezze, Monzu, Canteen, Commune, Commissary, and more. He himself began to eat healthier, eventually switching to vegan and raw foods for his own health, and it began to weigh on him that he was feeding others in his restaurants unhealthy foods laden with rich butter, cream, and fatty meats. His answer was to bring his award-winning chef skills to Oklahoma, where he's created a menu at **Matthew Kenney OKC** (p. 37) that's quite the opposite of his past ventures. But a restaurant alone is not enough for Chef Kenney; he also teaches students from all over the world to prepare raw cuisines at **Matthew Kenney Academy** (p. 53) one of the only raw food cooking schools in the world and located adjacent to the restaurant in a special test kitchen that can be viewed from the sidewalk through a floor-to-ceiling paned storefront.

without having dessert; it's delicious, raw, and (gasp) good for you. I always order the Hazelnut Chocolate Tart with Hazelnut Caramel, a decadent treat you'd never guess was healthy, but is! Their Juice Bar also offers up organic wines and smoothies and fresh juices.

Mutt's Amazing Hot Dogs, 1400 NW 23rd St., Paseo Arts District, Oklahoma City, OK 73106; (405) 525-3647; mutts-hot-dogs.com; Hot Dogs; $. "The dog pack" consists of co-owners and chefs Cally Johnson and Kathryn Mathis, who are also the creative minds behind another foodie favorite: Big Truck Tacos. These two ladies cook up some crazy dogs in many varieties such as chicken, duck, lobster, gator, and veggie. Try the higher-end dogs like the Pond Dog, a duck sausage topped with brie, caramelized apple, and onion, or an Ardee Dog, a Kobe beef dog combined with truffle aioli, potato salad, blue cheese, and fried onions. Or shoot for the delicious Hot Wing Dog, a chicken-fried chicken dog topped with green habañero sauce, blue cheese, and celery. Add an order of duck fat fries with truffle oil or fried pickles to finish it off.

Nic's Grill, 1201 N. Pennsylvania Ave, Oklahoma City, OK 73107; (405) 524-0999; Burgers; $. "Do one thing, and do it well" could be a motto on the staff workers' shirts at Nic's Grill, except they really do about four things well: burgers, fries, breakfast, and chicken-fried steak, but there is also something to be said for their daily lunch special of pork chops, meatloaf, or fried chicken. The burgers are monstrous so Nic doesn't offer a double and you probably couldn't handle it anyway! You may need to take your burgers to go as this place is tiny and without many seats, but the onion-fried burgers are good enough to make people wait! You can also grab a quick morning pick-me-up up of standard eggs, bacon, or sausage from their wildly popular breakfast menu. Go early for lunch to avoid the lines!

Paseo Grill, 2909 Paseo Dr., Paseo Arts District, Oklahoma City, OK 73103; (405) 601-1079; paseogrill.com; Steaks/Seafood; $$$. Step into Paseo Grill and also walk into a romantic delight of a place to dine. From the individually curtained booths, to the reading glasses scattered around on each lovely table to provide reading ease for the candlelight atmosphere, Joe Jungmann and Lesley Rawlinson have really paid attention to all the details it takes to make a lovely dining experience. Located in the heart of the Paseo Arts District, this little gem offers up a cream of mushroom soup that those who've moved out of state have shipped to them, a Chilean sea bass that drips with a citrus lime beurre blanc, delectable steaks and a prime rib eye and my personal favorite—their Southwest meat loaf. If you're around for lunch, don't miss out on their chicken potpie—it's one of the best in the city!

Pho Lien Hoa, 901 NW 23rd St., Paseo Arts District, Oklahoma City, OK 73106; (405) 521-8087; Vietnamese; $. Ask just about any *pho* lover in Oklahoma City where to go for the good stuff and they'll tell you Pho Lien Hoa. The king-daddy of all *pho* places, this is the foodie preference in Oklahoma City. Once only sporting a clientele of native Asians, word is quickly getting out that this place is fantastic. Authentic hot, steaming bowls of *pho* with no fuss are

Oklahoma Is Pho Crazy

Once only known in our Asian District (Little Saigon), where you can see multiple signs sporting "pho" in their names, *pho* has been sweeping across the Oklahoma City greater metro area and even extending into Edmond due to its great popularity. If you haven't experienced *pho,* it is a Vietnamese noodle soup that just oozes comfort food. Its steaming, fragrant broth is simmered for hours with wonderful things like star anise, cinnamon, cloves, and cardamom; the dish just pulls you in when you smell it. Also at the base of the broth are usually bones of some sort, like oxtail, that release their wonderful marrow flavor while simmering slowly. Add in some rice noodles, cilantro, and white and green onions, and then choose your protein, which ranges from thinly sliced brisket or steak, or venture into other meats like tendon, tripe, or meatballs. And to top it off, there is a large platter of herbs like Thai basil, or bean sprouts, lime, and jalapeño slices. Drizzle in some sriracha sauce, hoisin sauce, and perhaps a drop or two of fish sauce and you've got your taste buds dancing with joy. Try some *pho* in Oklahoma when you visit. You'll find yourself craving it on a bitter cold day, or just anytime.

whisked around the dining room in three sizes, small, large, and gigantic (extra large), and accompanied by large platters of fresh Thai basil, limes, jalapeño slices, bean sprouts, and sawleaf herb.

Pair it with a guacamole smoothie with tapioca balls to round out one unforgettable meal.

Picasso Cafe, 3009 Paseo Dr., Paseo Arts District, Oklahoma City, OK 73103; (405) 602-2002; picassosonpaseo.com; Cafe; $$. This local eatery is a hangout for the artsy crowd, those who love to sit on the patio, and those who love live bands (Wed through Sat). A room adjacent to the dining room has overstuffed couches to hang out and grab a drink and gab, and in fact, Picasso has a very loyal local fan base who stop by after work to do just that. I personally enjoy their pizzas best of all, and am fond of the prosciutto pizza with figs and blue cheese, but their pan-seared chicken in a bacon cream is also a favorite. They offer a nice vegetarian menu as well so if you're in the mood for something a little eclectic, and a little out of the ordinary, stop in to Picasso Cafe for a day . . . or a night out!

The Red Cup, 3122 N. Classen Blvd., Asian District, Oklahoma City, OK 73118; (405) 525-3430; redcupokc.com; Sandwiches/ Vegetarian; $. You may see some hippie folk at Red Cup or you may see some biker dudes, but one thing is certain, you'll get some tasty, healthy food. Want some organic coffee? Red Cup has it and try their Sexi Mexi, a chocolaty cinnamon espresso. How about loose-leaf tea, soy milk, or a smoothie? Yep, they have those as well. But drinks are only the beginning of your experience here. You won't see meat on the vegetarian menu, but Red Cup dishes up some wonderful flavor all the same. Try my favorite sandwich here: The Deuce. It's a toasted sesame bagel slathered with dilled cream cheese, avocado, and onion, and it's filling and delicious! The Red Cup also offers up some wonderful vegetarian breakfast offerings, and don't leave without trying one of their baked goods.

Red PrimeSteak, 504 N. Broadway Ave., Automobile Alley District, Oklahoma City, OK 73102; (405) 232-2626; redprimesteak .com; Steak House/Seafood; $$$$. Looking for a sleek ambience like 18-foot ceilings, red lighting, a towering floor-to-ceiling wine wall, and some truly unique fine dining? This is the place. Ask for a table near the Exhibition Kitchen and see how all the culinary magic goes down. Drool over one of their Wagyu center-cut rib eyes and pick a crust for it as well, including guajillo chile or brown sugar and sea salt. Also top your steak with one of their delectable sauces like roasted poblano chimichurri or black truffle butter. Red also has seafood offerings, or you can take a trip to the playful side and order Bacon Wrapped Bacon, a braised pork belly wrapped in hickory-smoked bacon. If you're a mac and cheese fan, don't miss out on their green chile mac. It's to die for.

Republic Gastropub, 5830 N. Classen Blvd., Belle Isle District, Oklahoma City, OK 73118; (405) 286-4577; republicgastropub.com; Gastropub; $$. The amazingly cool architecture will strike you first when you enter Republic Gastropub, and then you'll be impressed by the towering wall made of hundreds of bottles of every kind of beer imaginable. In fact there are 100 beers on tap and 250 bottled offerings available at this place. Part beer bar, part upscale American eatery, Republic throws subtle hints at its Irish heritage with fun snacks like Scotch eggs, poutine, and their house-made Pub Pretzel. Experience one of their house specialties like bock-battered fish-and-chips with capered tartar sauce. But in my opinion, their burgers are where it's at. Complete with homemade pretzel buns and fresh beef, their burgers are loved by everyone! And for dessert? You must try Meme's Donuts: warm spiced-sugar doughnuts with three dipping sauces (salted caramel, chocolate, and raspberry). Republic has a very sleek patio with giant flat screens for watching your favorite game alfresco on a nice night. See Executive Chef Donnie Cashion's recipe for **Pecan Coffee Cake** on p. 263.)

Rococo Restaurant & Fine Wine, 2824 N. Pennsylvania Ave., Oklahoma City, OK 73107; (405) 528-2830; rococo-restaurant.com; Seafood; $$$. Ask people for their take on Rococo Restaurant & Fine Wine, or simply Rococo's, and they'll mention the crab cakes, which some say are arguably the best in the city. This makes sense, and is true, but there is so much more than that at Rococo. Chef-Owner Bruce Rinehart, along with Executive Chef Don Duncan (at the Northpark location), offer up some unique things like "cookies," or bruschetta-type appetizers, sometimes served complimentary to his diners. Feast on the blue cheese cookie, with cream cheese and Parmesan in a perfect blend and spread over toasted bread and topped

Chef Spotlight: Bruce Rinehart

Chef Bruce Rinehart is one of the chefs most beloved by locals in Oklahoma City. He hails from New London, Connecticut, and is a chef who's been in the industry over 30 years. Bruce trained at the esteemed Hotel Del Coronado in San Diego and then worked his way up through small independents, corporate groups, hotels, and casinos. Bruce owned his first restaurant in Guilford, Connecticut, called Whitfield Alley, which opened in the early '90s to much acclaim. Indeed the *New York Times* called it a "glowing little bistro." From there Bruce went on to be the culinary director of Legal Seafood out of Boston. Relocating to Oklahoma in 2003 to give ownership another shot, Bruce has truly created a very special concept called Rococo. An "East Coast–style" restaurant with perhaps the best crab cake you'll ever have, it emphasizes fresh seafood, steaks, and chops, with a blend of Italian, Asian, and French influences. Rococo has two great locations here in OKC to relax by the fire and enjoy a glass of wine, great food, and friends. Bruce resides in Oklahoma City with his bride Amber and their two wonderful boys Will and Brak. Visit Rococo's and you're sure to chat with Bruce as he almost always makes rounds to visit his patrons during dinner.

with toasted garlic slivers and Asiago cheese. For a main course try my personal favorite: bamboo-steamed salmon that is steamed over a fragrant broth and served with stir-fried green cabbage, pea pods, scallions, carrots, wild mushrooms, and a special Asian glaze and sesame oil. If you dine, Bruce is sure to come around and talk to you. Those of us who know him know that he is one of the nicest guys in town. (See Bruce's recipe for **Sesame Vin Dressing** on p. 242) There is also a second location (and a wonderful cruise-style buffet on Sundays) at their Northpark location at 12252 N. May Ave., Oklahoma City, OK 73120; (405) 212-4577.

Saigon Baguette (Milk Bottle Building), 2426 N. Classen Blvd., Asian District, Oklahoma City, OK 73106; (405) 521-2660; Vietnamese; $. Located in the historic "Milk Bottle Building" (there is a giant Braum's milk bottle on top of the building) and featured recently in *Southern Living* magazine, Saigon Baguette makes arguably the best *banh mi* sandwich in the city. Step into the tiny waiting room and order your sandwich to go; they are unbelievably delicious and inexpensive. They also offer some fresh spring rolls with peanut sauce that are superb as well and you can grab a cold Asian drink out of the cooler, including soda, mango juice, coconut juice, and more!

Sushi Neko, 4318 N. Western Ave., Western Avenue District, Oklahoma City, OK 73118; (405) 528-8862; sushineko.com; Japanese/Sushi; $$$. Sushi Neko is a trendy and swanky sushi bar that always seems to have a line out the door. From its patio tables with umbrellas to its retro Asian decor inside, it is just a happening place to hang out. While waiting on your sushi, try a lobster shooter—lobster chunks bathed in red curry coconut sauce or their spicy miso soup with green mussels, shrimp, and scallops. Dining

here for lunch? Try the Sushi Deluxe with assorted pieces of nigiri sushi selected by the chef and some rolled pieces as well. For dinner try the Boatload of Sushi or the Sushi Party Boat with a mix of sashimi and rolls. Venture off the sushi menu and try an entree by ordering the Cherry Blossom Beef Tenderloin, a 10-ounce fillet crusted with peppercorns and sauced with a lovely mix of Cabernet and cherries. Round out the evening with creamy and delicious vanilla bean coconut panna cotta.

Tucker's Onion Burgers, 324 NW 23rd St., Paseo Arts District, Oklahoma City, OK 73103; (405) 609-2333; tuckersonionburgers .com; Burgers; $. Many years ago in Oklahoma, around the Great Depression, restaurants decided to stretch their buck by adding onions to their burgers when they tossed them on the flat grill. The onion burger was invented and has stuck with us here ever since. And Tucker's is a great place to go get one! Their small but gratifying menu consists of a single or double premium onion burger hand-formed from fresh meat from Creekstone Farms right here in Oklahoma. There is also a turkey burger that is perhaps the best I've had at a restaurant. But then, there's the "Mother Tucker," which is over 1 pound of fried onion burger goodness (triple beef and onions). Tuckers also does french fries well, hand cutting them and serving them up hot and crispy. Don't forget to get a hand-scooped milk shake or a strawberry limeade. Tucker's also offers canned beer.

Upper Crust, 5860 N. Classen Blvd., Belle Isle District, Oklahoma City, OK 73118; (405) 842-7743; okcbestpizza .com; Pizza; $$. With its hip red leather seats, brick wall mixed with towering glass windows, streamlined Classen Curve architectural design, and granite-topped bar, Upper Crust is a happening place to go and grab a pizza. You can pick out a bottle of wine by climbing up the sliding ladder in the walk-in wine room all the while taking in whiffs of the pecan, hickory, and oak wood–fired pizzas. Start off with some smoky wood-fired long stem artichokes. Then get ready and build your own pizza with such ingredients as "fire-roasted pie sauce," Texas goat cheese, capocollo ham, bricked chicken, shaved fennel, or capers. Or you can order one of their artisan-style pies. Finish it all off with a cookie pie, a 50/50 mix of two luscious cookie doughs served warm and topped off with vanilla bean ice cream.

The Wedge Pizzeria, 4709 NW Western Ave., Western Avenue District, Oklahoma City, OK 73118; (405) 602-3477; Gourmet Pizza; $$. This quaint little neighborhood pizza joint oozes pizza and foodie passion. From the gardens out back that supply some of their fresh herbs, to the smoked pecan wood, to the bustling waitstaff, you always feel like you're at home. In the evenings take a pick from their wonderful assortment of beers, several of which are locally handcrafted by Oklahoma brewers, or enjoy a nice glass of wine (their Deep Deuce location offers a full bar). For starters, try the antipasto, an enormous platter of roasted seasonal vegetables and fruit that changes according to what's available locally. It's also piled with *salumi,* spiced nuts, and gourmet cheeses. Don't forget to check the chalkboard to the right of the bar for their seasonal selection of bruschetta offerings. My favorite pizza is the Truffle Shuffle pizza, with homemade crust, roasted chicken, cremini mushrooms, spinach, Parmesan, and mozzarella, all drizzled with white truffle oil. Dine on their twinkle-lit patio or play bocce ball in the garden. The Wedge also has a second location at its Deep Deuce digs at 230 NE 1st Street, Oklahoma City, OK 73104; (405)270-0660.

Landmarks

Jamil's Steakhouse, 4910 N. Lincoln Blvd., Oklahoma City, OK 73105; jamilssteakhouseokc.com; Lebanese Steak House; $$$. Open for more than 50 years, Jamil's has a dedicated clientele and new visitors who are pleasantly surprised. This old-time steak house is the first place my husband and I ever danced, to romantic, old-school Frank Sinatra music, when we first dated. Don't expect typical appetizers here—you will receive the staple relish plate of veggie sticks along with hummus, tabouleh, and, my favorite, a basket of barbecue ribs and bologna. The thick-sliced and grilled bologna brings back happy memories as does the *malfouf* (cabbage rolls stuffed with cinnamon-scented rice and meat). Move on to the star of the show: the steaks. Splurge on either the porterhouse, the rib eye or the filet.

Leo's BBQ, 3631 N. Kelley Ave., Downtown District, Oklahoma City, OK 73111; (405) 424-5367; Barbecue; $. Recently featured on *Diners, Drive-Ins and Dives,* this place has been getting new attention (although we locals have known about it for a long time). First, and most important: Do not leave without having some strawberry banana cake. If you do, you'll regret it because Leo's offers a slice of their family recipe cake with every dinner at Leo's for free and it is an Oklahoma favorite. Charles Smith has been serving up hickory-smoked meat since 1974. Charles only serves up spareribs at his place—you won't find any baby back ribs here. But there are also hot links, BBQ bologna (my favorite!), chicken, and moist, tender, smoked brisket. Ladle on some of the sauce he cooks for two days and enjoy some lip-smacking side dishes like macaroni salad, potato salad, and baked beans.

Specialty Stores, Markets & Producers

Beans & Leaves, 4015 N. Pennsylvania Ave. Ste. B, Oklahoma City, OK 73112; (405) 604-4700. Nestled in a little strip center, Beans & Leaves' coffee is amazing. The atmosphere is fun and hip and barista Gary will make you a fantastic drink upon request. Try one of their amazing desserts like upside-down pumpkin pie, or the key lime cheesecake. A must-try is the orange spice tea latte, popular with the foodie crowd.

Cuppies and Joe, 727 NW 23rd St., Paseo Arts District, Oklahoma City, OK 73103; (405) 528-2122; cuppiesandjoe.com. Here is the perfect equation for success: Buy an old house with various levels, redo it with vintage furniture and cozy, eclectic groupings, and start a family coffee/cupcake shop in it. That's exactly what the Diefenderfer family has done on 23rd Street. The locally roasted coffee is by Elemental, and they also serve one of the best lattes or chai lattes in town. Hang out in the vintage rooms with unmatched couches, tables, and armchairs while eating some of their signature flavors. Flavors change daily so take note of the website if you're planning on visiting! If you're lucky enough to get them before they're sold out, try the Horsebite carrot cupcake with cream-cheese frosting or the Boom Boom Pow, a vanilla-bean cuppie with chocolate buttercream with a little nest of caramel on the top and sprinkled with sea salt. Also try one of their homemade pies like apple praline or Lemon Luscious.

Forward Foods, 5123 N. Western Ave., Western Avenue District, Oklahoma City, OK 73118; (405) 879-9937; forwardfoods.com. This is your go-to local grocery for wonderful items like speck, Serrano ham, fresh produce, finishing salts, and more. From their huge lineup of local products to imported Italian pastas, olive oils, and vanilla (you can fill your own bottles with these), Forward Foods is a great little gourmet market. They have a wonderful olive bar with other offerings like preserved lemons and caper berries, and I love to pick up a carton of local free-range eggs from Oklahoma-based

Walnut Creek Farms each time I'm there. But the true prize at Forward Foods is the cheese case. They offer over 200 varieties of delectable cheeses like Beeler gruyère and *chèvre noir* by Tournevent, and the glass case always makes me smile with joy to see it. The market also houses a small cafe where you can get items like soup, quiche, or sandwiches, so drop in, grab a bite to eat, and maybe take some heirloom dried beans or lentils to go! There is a second location at 2001 W. Main St., Ste. 111, Norman, OK 73069; (405) 321-1007.

OSU-OKC Farmers' Market, 200 N. Portland Ave., Oklahoma City, OK 73107 (OSU-OKC college campus Horticulture Pavilion). Visit this quaint, ever-growing farmers' market on Sat from 10 a.m. to 1 p.m. in the winter or from 8 a.m. to 1 p.m. in the summer (it is also open in the summer on Wed from 11 to 4 p.m.). You'll find fresh produce, dairy, eggs, meats, and many more local Oklahoma goods like buffalo meat, yogurt cream cheese from Wagon Creek Dairy, and, in the summer, all kinds of fresh vegetables.

Super Cao Nguyen Asian Market, 2668 N. Military Ave., Asian District, Oklahoma City, OK 73106; (405) 525-7652; caonguyen .com. Need some lemongrass, beech mushrooms, six kinds of house-made kimchee, or maybe some Thai basil? How about the best ahi tuna, whole red snapper, or fresh blue crabs? Cao Nguyen

Asian Market is your place. Browse their produce for Chinese garlic chives, baby bok choy, or long beans, or saunter down their endless meat counter with some of the best fish available and hard-to-find meats like oxtail or live Manila clams. Cao Nguyen has an aisle for every Asian culture with imported bottled sauces and packages from Japan to Thailand. They even carry *balut* duck eggs, if you wish to try them. Or if you're looking for Asian dishware or cookware, there are endless aisles of sushi sets, mortars and pestles, bamboo steamers, and the like. Make sure you have plenty of time so you can browse slowly and take it all in.

Learn to Cook

Matthew Kenney Academy, 5820 N. Classen Blvd., Belle Isle District, Ste. 1, Oklahoma City, OK 73118; (405) 842-1050; matthewkenneycuisine.com/education. When visiting Matthew Kenney Academy, I met students from all over the country and around the world. These students are eager to come and be tutored by the master of raw food and learn how to prepare delicious dishes like beet gnocchi and black and white kimchee dumplings. Using whole, organic, unprocessed plant-based foods, this state-licensed academy prepares those wanting to cook in the raw-food manner or any chef wishing to expand his or her repertoire of cuisine. The beautiful, tall, glass-windowed exterior of the Academy allows passersby to watch the chefs-in-training at work. You can become raw-food-chef certified by taking their 1- to 2-month training or you can enroll in a 1-night course that features a specific aspect of raw cuisine, like making fresh cheese. The classes change frequently so you can go time and time again. See the website for details.

NW Oklahoma City, Nichols Hills/ Lakeside & Edmond

The Northwest Oklahoma City area is a newer area of Oklahoma City and, heading into Edmond, one of the fastest-growing areas for new housing and restaurants around. While these areas house many businesses, rural neighborhoods, and chain restaurants, there are also many local places continually cropping up as well, and worth visiting if you're coming to OKC.

Ranging from the 39th Street Bethany/Warr Acres area all the way up to Memorial Avenue and NW Expressway, Northwest Oklahoma City has many offerings that are must-tries. There is a large concentration of Hispanic/Latin culture here from markets to restaurants. This should come as no great surprise when one realizes Oklahoma's close proximity to Mexico. What this means in a nutshell is there are some absolutely amazing eateries featuring

Latin, Spanish, and Mexican influences in Oklahoma City as a result of this migration northward.

The Lakeside District of Oklahoma City is named after its close proximity to Lake Hefner, which sits smack dab in the center of Oklahoma City. This lake sports motorboats and also scads of sailboats on nice days, and it was only natural that East Wharf dining restaurants would crop up. Boaters can pull up to courtesy docks on the East Wharf and head up to dine or even call ahead and have food delivered down to the dock. But this district also encompasses the Nichols Hills area with streets like May Avenue, Pennsylvania Avenue, and Western Avenue as well, with its unique shops and places to dine.

What began as a water and coaling station for steam engines in the late 1800s is now one of the most happening cities in Oklahoma. Beginning on the northern border of Oklahoma City, and with US Highway 77 (Broadway Extension) and I-35 access, Edmond was included on CNBC's "10 Perfect Suburbs" list. It also houses one of the largest farmers' markets around and has an abundance of local eateries from one end of its border to the other, including several in its business district and also some fun eateries around the University of Central Oklahoma.

Foodie Faves

Abel's Mexican Restaurant, 5822 NW 50th St., NW Oklahoma City, Oklahoma City, OK 73122; (405) 491-0911; Mexican; $$. This brightly painted building is hard to miss as you drive down 50th Street in NW Oklahoma City and besides, if you did miss it, you'd be sorry! If you can handle the heat, try the *botana* to start. Grilled onions and jalapeño peppers mashed up with tomatoes and served with avocado slices make it hard to stop eating this flaming-hot salsa-meets-guacamole. Check out their wall board in the front room for off-menu items like gorditas. Try the 7 Mares Soup, chock-full of things like crab claws, octopus, catfish, shrimp, white clams, and mussels all in steaming spicy broth and served with rice. Look for the silver-haired man with the swirly mustache because he frequents the dining room—say hi to Abel the owner and the namesake of the restaurant. Dine at Abel's and you'll find out why Oklahoma City locals drive northwest from all over just to feast on this cuisine.

Birrieria Diaz, 6700 NW 39th Expy., NW Oklahoma City, Bethany, OK 73008; (405) 603-1304; Mexican; $. Want something authentically Mexican and not standard, sloppy enchiladas that have been so Americanized they are just blah? Try Birrieria Diaz. This gem of a restaurant is tucked away in downtown Bethany and is full of home-cooked family love. The specialty of the eatery is *birria,* a Guadalajara dish not usually seen around these parts. Order the *birria* in lamb or beef, and I highly recommend the sheep, so be brave and try it out. It's a slow-cooked stew of roasted peppers and spices that comes out served with house-made tortillas—some grilled and crispy and some steamed. Pay attention to the board at the front of the small dining room and try out some of the dishes listed. The *huaraches* are spectacular oblong fried masa pillows (*sopes*) topped with a beans, meat, cilantro, onions, *queso fresco*, and lettuce, and drizzled with sour cream. Sip a Mexican imported beer or a real Mexican Coca-Cola to cool down your tongue.

Boulevard Steakhouse, 505 S. Boulevard St., Edmond, OK 73034; boulevardsteakhouse.com; Steak House; $$$$. Around for nearly 15 years, Boulevard Steakhouse has always been known as a special place to go. Owners Peter and Sheree Holloway offer up a luxurious setting with brick walls and glowing chandeliers along with white tablecloths, richly wood-hued ceilings and a wine cellar to make anyone happy. Sit in the cigar lounge if you're a manly man or experience the Wine Room dining area. Wherever you end up, it's pure elegance. The big star on the starter menu is the portobello mushroom soup. Some argue that the rib eye at Boulevard is the best in town and all their steaks are prime aged beef that tends to melt in your mouth. The sides at Boulevard are generous—be sure to share with the rest of the table! Of notable mention is the lobster macaroni and the creamed spinach and oh my . . . the au gratin potatoes. They also have a wonderful prix-fixe menu for large parties so check it out on their website. Fancy yourself a wine lover? Boulevard is your place. (See Chef Jimmy Stepney's recipe for **Tomato & Herb Tart** on p. 243.)

Brown Bag Deli, 7600 N. Western Ave., Nichols Hills District, Oklahoma City, OK 73116; (405) 842-1444; Deli; $. Simple, wonderful ingredients make this one of my favorite places to grab a sandwich. I dream about the chicken sandwich: Slices of a whole chicken breast are tucked into a pita-type pocket and piled full of sprouts, tomato slices, onion, and a homemade herbed mayonnaise that makes me want more. The chicken salad is flavored with curry powder and is out of this world. For a special treat, have it served in avocado halves instead of on bread and get a side order of hummus to go with it. And listen carefully when I tell you to get one of their lemon squares. The rich, creamy tart squares will make your eyes roll backward in joy!

Bunny's Onion Burgers, 5020 N. Meridian Ave., NW Oklahoma City, Oklahoma City, OK 73112; (405) 949-2889; bunnysonionburger .com; Burgers; $. The original Bunny's was a Tastee Freeze opened in 1955, then switched to Joe's Onion Burgers, and in 1990, became Bunny's under original owner Bunny Biggers. Sold in 2008 to owners Bobby Hawkins and Bill Burnett, Bunny's Onion Burgers is a no-fuss, tiny little place where most people take their grub to go because there are only a few scattered tables inside. There are, however, some seats around the counter where you can watch them sling fresh ground beef, American cheese, and thinly sliced onions onto a flat grill and cook up deliciousness. The double and triple burgers

THE FIRST HAMBURGER

Did you know that some argue that the first hamburger served on a bun was made by Oscar Weber Bilby of Tulsa, Oklahoma, in 1891? It's true. The discovery was made while Michael Wallis, a Route 66 expert, was researching the state's juiciest and most delectable hamburgers. He started by checking out Tulsa's most highly praised burger—at Weber's Root Beer Stand. His results? Mr. Wallis found that Oscar Weber Bilby was the first person to serve a real hamburger! On Independence Day (what better day for the burger to be invented?), 1891, beef in ground form was served on his wife's homemade buns at a party held at his farm. Up until that point Athens, Texas, was credited with the invention of the burger, but we believe that to be false because it was served on slices of bread, a format commonly known as a "patty melt" and certainly not a burger!

In April 1995, Oklahoma Governor Frank Keating corrected all wrongs. He proclaimed that the first true hamburger on a bun was first grilled up in Tulsa, Oklahoma, in 1891. The Governor's Proclamation on April 13, 1995, cites Tulsa as "The Real Birthplace of the Hamburger."

are ample appetite pleasers and the onion rings are crisp outside and nicely softened inside. Once you have a Bunny's burger, you'll find yourself reminiscing about it time and time again. There is a second location at 1023 S. Meridian Ave., Oklahoma City, OK 73108; (405) 949-2949.

Cajun King, 5816 NW 63rd St., NW Oklahoma City, Oklahoma City, OK 73132; (405) 603-3714; cajunkingokc.com; Cajun/Creole; $$. Here in Oklahoma, we take our fried catfish seriously. So the first time I visited Cajun King, the creation of Louisiana natives Ken Mills and Simeon Adda, I was sold. The concept of Cajun King is simple: Pay at the door and eat all you want off the buffet filled with New Orleans goodness. I've learned what I like, and I like the greens, the crawfish étouffée and the blackened chicken pasta. Oh, and there's fried chicken the likes of none you've had before. Scented with cinnamon, this fried chicken is highly addictive! Upon returning to your table, you'll find a plate piled high with fried catfish, and I guarantee it's the best catfish you've ever had. The good news? They keep on bringing the catfish . . . until you say stop. Along with the catfish, your server will also bring an endless supply of beignets, hot, crispy, and dusted with powdered sugar. Go on Saturday and try some specialties like gator and dumplings and fried boudin balls (stuffed sausage balls). They've opened a second location at 700 Ed Noble Pkwy., Norman, OK 73072; (405) 928-5050.

Charm Restaurant, 5805 NW 50th St., NW Oklahoma City, Oklahoma City, OK 73122; (405) 792-2153; Thai; $$. You know you've found a good Thai sauce when you spend your time analyzing how you can make it at home. Such is the case whenever I eat at Charm. The Thai basil is my healthy choice and it is chock full of fresh veggies like onions, red pepper, green pepper, jalapeño slices, and mushrooms. Order it with chicken or tofu and it comes out surrounded by the most delectable brown sauce. The Rama Chicken also has a delectable sauce that packs a bit of heat and sweetness all in one. Want a steaming bowl of soup goodness? Try the Boat Noodle Soup with a cinnamon-scented broth and packed with beef, rice noodles, bean sprouts, green onions, and garlic. In the hot summer, I love the cool version of *larb kai* salad. Minced chicken pieces accompanied by a julienned salad of cabbage, carrot, mint, and cilantro are drizzled in a lime-based spicy fish sauce and mixed with slivered red onions.

Cow Calf Hay, 3409 Wynn Dr., Edmond, OK 73103; (405) 509-2333; facebook.com/pages/The-Cow-Calf-Hay; Burgers; $. Seriously wacky cow-inspired decor adds to the funky atmosphere when you go to the Cow Calf Hay. The decor is also accompanied by some seriously good burgers. The small menu means one thing—good burgers done well and a few sides that are exceptional. All of Cow's burgers are made with fresh certified Angus beef chuck and they are truly among the best burgers in town. I swoon over the Barnyard Burger, topped with sautéed mushrooms, pepper jack cheese, grilled onions, and a flavorful garlic mayonnaise and served on a crispy bun that's been grilled in butter. They also have a mean turkey burger and also a garden veggie patty burger that is made with a blend of veggies like mushrooms, water chestnuts, brown rice, black olives, and rolled oats and capped off with a spicy ranch dressing. Make sure you try the onion rings and for dessert, try the Cow Pie Cake, a piece of yellow cake that's been drizzled with strawberry juice, topped with whipped cream, then covered with fresh bananas and strawberry sauce.

El Pollo Chulo, 5805 NW 50th St., NW Oklahoma City, Oklahoma City, OK 73122; (405) 792-2300; elpollochulo.com; Spanish; $. "Succulent" is the word that comes to mind when you describe the chicken at El Pollo Chulo. Spatchcocked, marinated in fruit and lime juices, and cooked over a large grill, these chickens will have you salivating as soon as you walk in and see them on the grill. Criminal not to start with the chicken, but move on to other menu items, like the grilled salmon or the Baja fish tacos and you won't be disappointed. The sign on the wall boasts "We worry about what goes into your body so you don't have to" and you leave this place feeling no guilt whatsoever yet very satisfied. I am a big fan of the Pollo Bowls, especially the "Big O," where tasty chicken is incorporated into bowls filled with pinto beans, Spanish rice, and shredded pepper jack cheese and fresh guacamole. Coming in at under a measly four bucks, you just can't beat this.

Flatire Burgers, 318 E. Ayers St., Edmond, OK 73034; (405) 359-2006; flatireburgers.com; Burgers; $. Ask anyone who lives in Edmond what their favorite eatery is and you're sure to hear an outcry of "Flatire Burgers"! Located across from the University of Central Oklahoma, this burger joint surprises with their innovative menu that offers up things like the Hell's Kitchen Burger or the Reuben Burger (corned beef, kraut, and swiss on top of a burger) or for avocado lovers, how about the Guacamole Burger? And just because it's the Southwest, how about having your burger on a jalapeño bun? And if you want something other than a burger, try the fish tacos piled high with shredded cabbage and spiced up with sriracha sauce. Try the hot and crispy sweet potato fries—if you're a sweets freak get them covered in cinnamon sugar, but I prefer them savory and sprinkled with a hint of salt. For dessert? Order the S'mores Experience. They'll bring out a small grill with s'mores fixings to grill right at your table!

Gopuram Taste of India, 4559 NW 23rd St., NW Oklahoma City, Oklahoma City, OK 73127; (405) 948-7373; gopuramtasteofindia .com; Indian; $$. Step into Gopuram and you will feel like you've been transported to India. The decor is beautiful, the dining room spacious, and the buffet is large and surprisingly tasty for a . . . well, buffet. Go on a Friday night and visit the large banquet room reserved especially for belly dancing. Menu favorites are the heavily spiced tandoori chicken and the naan, which your server will bring out piping hot to your table. However, I do visit the buffet for the fried, breaded spinach, which is highly addictive. I also love the mango pudding on the dessert bar, a thin custard full of flavor that really cools down your mouth after eating some of the spicier dishes.

Hefner Grill, 9201 Lake Hefner Pkwy., Lakeside District, Oklahoma City, OK 73120; (405) 748-6113; hefnergrill.com; Steaks/Seafood; $$. Feel like dining on the waterfront? Want to sit on a patio overlooking Lake Hefner? Want to listen to some fabulous music with your sweetheart? You must visit Hefner Grill. Visit at lunch and try the Baltimore crab dip. Scoop up the cream cheese mixed with lump crab with some tortilla chips that's been sprinkled with green onions. Slurp up some oysters on the half shell or try the Tabasco Caesar salad. At dinner, sample the seafood enchiladas filled with shrimp, scallops, and mushrooms and smothered in a wonderful warm ancho cream sauce. But our favorite time to visit is Sunday brunch where we love to feast on the Southern Eggs Benedict. A fried green tomato, crispy and savory, sits atop a corn cake and is topped with a slice of smoked grilled ham. Next comes a poached egg and some fire-roasted guacamole and a light drizzling of spiced hollandaise sauce. It's one of our favorites at Hefner Grill while listening to Justin Echols sing his smooth jazz and tickle the baby grand piano at the bar.

Home Run Sliders, 128 East 5th St., Edmond, OK 73034; (405) 513-5410; homerunsliders.com; Burgers; $. Sometimes good things do come in small packages. Take for instance the slider at Home Run Sliders. Three ounces of pure fresh beef sits inside a split-top roll and topped with things like candied blackened bacon and blue cheese crumbles. Or how about trying the Barn Burner, a slider topped with spicy Tabasco rings and hot wing sauce? If you're looking for an option besides ground beef, try the Mighty Glove slider, with pecan-crusted chicken, chipotle aioli, and jicama slaw. They also make a pretty good veggie burger in the Mean Green, topped with grilled onions and honey mustard sauce. And I couldn't go without mentioning the fries, Tater Tots, and ketchup bar. Home Run Sliders has sweet potato and regular fries that are darn good and you also get to try the ketchup bar with over a dozen or more flavors of gourmet ketchup like ancho chile, ranch, theta (an Oklahoma City burger preference of hickory sauce, mayonnaise, cheese, and pickles), or Dr. Pepper ketchups. Wash it down with a pineapple tea.

Humble Pie Pizzeria, 1319 S. Broadway, Edmond, OK 73034; (405) 715-1818; humblepie.com; Pizza; $$. Having lived near Chicago, I am a sucker for Chicago-style pizza and I'm always on the lookout for places that might live up to the original. Humble Pie comes doggone close and it is good, folks. Notice the dollar bills hanging from the ceiling, which the eatery donates toward O.A.T.H. (a human trafficking rescue group). From the "humble" (pun intended) outside façade in a strip mall to watching them make the pizza through the kitchen window, this place is just plain fun. Start out by ordering the Bottomless Pretzels. They're seasoned with a tad of spice and a touch of savory and are extremely addictive. The pizzas are offered in two styles, Chicago deep dish or thin New York style, and both are incredible. Check them out on Facebook for their "secret menu" and get even more choices, like The Kaiser, which was offered for a recent Oktoberfest; it featured five cheeses, smoked kielbasa, and sauerkraut. If you're looking for a healthier option, Humble Pie also offers some great salads to keep you fit as well.

Inspirations Tea Room, 2118 W. Edmond Rd., Edmond, OK 73003; (404) 715-2525; inspirationstearoom.com; Tea/Cafe; $$. If you want to go to this ladylike eatery, make sure you call ahead and make a reservation (ask for the gazebo table for a party of eight). It's always full and for good reason. From the homemade scones served complimentary with lemon curd to the gorgeous china, my girls and I make sure to come here every single time my mom comes into town. Order the Tea Party Tray and you'll be presented with a three-tiered tray of goodies from tea sandwiches, quiche, fresh fruit, and pastries, then order your pick of their delicious selection of loose-leaf teas, brewed into small pots and poured by your server. For the little girls, order the Princess Tea Party for One with a smaller tiered tray of darling, child-friendly tea sandwiches like heart-shaped peanut butter and marshmallow. Don't forget to visit the lovely tea shop before you leave.

Irma's Burgers, 1035 NW 63rd St., NW Oklahoma City, Oklahoma City, OK 73116; (405) 840-4672; Burgers; $. I love those places that make you feel like you're in an old-fashioned diner. Why? Because those places characteristically have fabulous food, and Irma's is no exception to the rule. Paneled walls, red vinyl booths, and old farmhouse-style cupboards full of slices of pie fit the bill. And the burgers? They're good, folks. The What U Lookin @ Burger boasts no bun, but instead sandwiches its meat (and a slew of other things) between two full grilled cheese sandwiches. Irma's also offers a pretty good dog as well called the Mannie's Famous Slaw Dog served with chili and old-fashioned spicy mustard slaw with a hint of sweetness. Irma's fries are hand cut and you can get a few varieties of them topped with things like the Benda's Favorite Fries, smothered in chipotle ranch and bacon. For dessert, try the buttermilk pie, an old southern staple custard-style pie that gives you just enough sweet to satisfy your appetite, if you still have one after that burger! There is a second location at 1120 Classen Dr., Oklahoma City, OK 73103; (405) 235-4762.

Khazana, 4900 N. May Ave., Lakeside District, Oklahoma City, OK 73112; (405) 948-6606; Indian; $$. Khazana's buffet is not unlike many other buffets you'll find at Indian restaurants. Most people don't stray too far past the buffet but in this case, I'd recommend you pick up a menu. Especially if you're a vegetarian. Their vegetarian clay pots are wonderful like the *channa masala* or garbanzo beans with a rich masala sauce. The biryanis are also excellent. Try the *murgh biryani* with its scrumptious saffron-infused rice and tender chunks of chicken and order a fresh order of garlic naan, instead of relying on the stuff drying out on the buffet. Brought hot to your table, you won't regret it. The one thing I'd miss about the buffet? The deep-fried breaded spinach. I just love that stuff to death. Good news though, you can order it fresh from the appetizer menu (spinach pakora) for a mere $3 and have your very own without worrying about sharing! And as always the tikka masala is fantastic at Khazana and always a good dish to try if you're an Indian newbie.

Kolache Kitchen, 5587 NW Expy., NW Oklahoma City, Oklahoma City, OK 73132; (405)720-7566, Kolaches; $. In case you don't know, *kolaches* are little pillows of puffy dough that have some sort of filling. Originally more dessert-like and fruit filled, as they got more popular, folks starting filling them with all sorts of savory ingredients like meat, cheese, and even eggs for breakfast. Try a sweet fruit-filled one for less than a buck, like key lime, blackberry or for pure deliciousness, try the poppy seed. Its sweet filling is delicious. For the heartier appetite, try one with sausage, egg, cheese, and jalapeño for breakfast or try the lunch variety like the turkey club. The lunch *kolaches* are the stuffed variety and the dough surrounds the filling and is baked. And here's the kicker: There is a sushi chef at this establishment from 11 a.m. to 8 p.m. and the sushi is pretty doggone good. They even offer a Lifesaver Roll stuffed with bacon! The dining room is tiny but you can always pick up a bag to go.

Lemongrass Thai, 253 S. Santa Fe Ave., Edmond, OK 73003; (405) 330-6888; lemongrassok.com; Thai; $$. The decor at Lemongrass is a little nicer than at many Thai restaurants around, and the food is so delicious. Indulge in their *tom kha* soup, with rich coconut broth, galangal, lemongrass, kaffir lime, mushrooms, onions, and lime juice. The balance of sweet, sour, savory, and

Home-Grown Chains: Hideaway Pizza

Richard and Marti Dermer opened the very first Hideaway Pizza restaurant in Stillwater, Oklahoma, in 1957 near the Oklahoma State University Campus. VW Bugs drove around delivering these pizzas to college students who needed a "hideaway" from studying. Oklahoma has loved them ever since. This fun-loving place serves up some wonderful pies including the Big Country, made for meat lovers with a healthy appetite, as it's chock-full of meats like pepperoni, Canadian bacon, Polish sausage, and hamburger with a generous helping of cheddar cheese and mozzarella. Want a more gourmet twist? Try the Mediterranean. Instead of pizza sauce, this one is glazed with olive oil and garlic and is topped with fresh spinach, mozzarella, and feta cheese and sprinkled with sun-dried tomatoes. However, my personal favorite is the Pizza of the Gods, once again with the garlic olive oil glaze but this time topped with smoked provolone, mozzarella, Roma tomatoes, artichoke hearts, and sliced mushrooms. If you're not in the pizza mood, Hideaway also offers up some good baked pasta dishes like Pasta Supreme, baked penne loaded up with pepperoni, sausage, mushrooms, green peppers, and onions. And don't leave without trying the sinful Warm Giant Chocolate Chip Cookie with a chocolate syrup drizzle. Check out their website (hideawaypizza.com) for more area location information.

spicy is the perfect Thai blend that it should be. All of the curries at Lemongrass are worth trying at least once. I am especially fond of the Jungle Curry, which is chock-full of all sorts of vegetables and your choice of chicken, tofu, shrimp, or beef. For those with a high tolerance for heat, order up the spicy green fried rice with a green curry paste stirred right into the rice as it fries. You can't go wrong with anything at Lemongrass Thai. As a bonus, they have a small wine list as well!

Mama E's Wings & Waffles, 3838 Springlake Dr., Oklahoma City, OK 73111; (405) 424-0800; Southern; $$. Need some serious soul food in Oklahoma City? Mama E's is the place. Housed in a small shack-type building, it may be small, but it delivers on flavor. Their specialty is chicken and waffles and they do it perfectly. From the crispy breaded chicken that sits atop a melt-in-your-mouth waffle, to the dusting of powdered sugar to finish it all off, they are a must-try. But if you want to venture past their namesake dish, try the wonderful greens and the mac and cheese, which is nothing to shake a stick at either. Got a big appetite? Go for the Soul Food Daily Special with choice of two meats, three sides, choice of roll or cornbread, dessert (their sweet potato pie gets my vote), and refillable Kool-Aid, just for the kid that you know is still inside of you.

Nhinja Sushi & Wok, 13905 N. May Ave., NW Oklahoma City, Oklahoma City, OK 73134; (405) 463-6622; nhinja.com; Sushi/ Japanese; $. Need some sushi quick and at a reasonable price? Nhinja Sushi & Wok may be the answer. Bright, airy, and retro Asian, bright punches of color accentuate the otherwise pristine atmosphere and you can have sushi or some really good wok dishes for under $10. Owners Kang and Mary Nhin wanted to open a place that is family-friendly with some healthy and delicious food that is served up fast. Our favorite rolls are the Geisha roll with tempura shrimp, avocado, cream cheese, tempura flakes, spicy mayo, and eel sauce. We love the crunch, creaminess, and spice. We also love the Nhinja roll with salmon, cream cheese, jalapeño, scallions, spicy mayo, and sesame seeds. The sushi is good and decently priced if you're craving it, but the wok dishes are what we come for again and again. Try the Hunan Garden Wok'd which is full of fresh vegetables like broccoli, mushrooms, snap peas, baby corn, and zucchini, and is bathed in a delicious soy garlic house sauce. Nhinja is a great quick stop fast-food sushi and wok place to grab some better than average Asian food on the run.

Nunu's Mediterranean Cafe and Market, 3131-B W. Memorial Rd., NW Oklahoma City, Oklahoma City, OK 73134; (405) 751-7000; nunuscafe.com; Mediterranean; $$. Nunu's is a fairly new Mediterranean eatery under the care of Nunu Farhood and is inspired, like many of us, by her mother's unbeatable cooking. Mama's cooking included things like *kefta,* lentil soup and *fatoosh.* From their incomparable falafel to their famous Cedar's Po'boy,

Nunu's motto is "make it like you'd make it at home." Dine in a modern Mediterranean-type setting or alfresco on their patio.

Queen of Sheba, 2308 MacArthur Blvd., NW Oklahoma City, Oklahoma City, OK 73127; (405) 606-8616; ethiopianrestaurant.com; Ethiopian; $$. Take a group or come with a date and experience Ethiopia when you walk in the doors of Queen of Sheba. From the decor to the music to the delicious food, you are transported into Ethiopian culture. Start off with their sweet honey wine, and move on to the Queen of Sheba platter for the best experience. This is an enormous platter covered with spongy injera bread with a sampling of salad, chickpeas, and lentils (*yesimir watt*), lamb (*yebeg alitcha*), chicken (*yedir watt*) and beef (*kay watt*) along with sautéed green beans. No silverware is needed. Pick up the items by tearing off a piece of the injera bread and use it to scoop up each flavorful bite. There are many offerings for vegetarians here as well. Let owner Mimi Younis prepare the Ethiopian coffee ceremony for you, which involves the roasting, grinding, and drinking of the coffee. But if you desire the ceremony, contact the restaurant 24 hours in advance.

Ranch Steakhouse, 3000 W. Britton Rd., Lakeside District, Oklahoma City, OK 73120; (405) 755-3501; ranchsteakhouse.com; Steak House/Seafood; $$$$. Softly lit dining rooms beckon you in as do the rustic wood walls adorned with classic western paintings and cozy leather seating. But that's where the homey feel ends, because this isn't home cooking. This is fine gourmet dining at its best, and the steaks at the Ranch don't need to be doctored up too much, because the dry-aged prime beef cuts are just that good and brought in locally from Premium Natural Beef in Hobart, Oklahoma. However, if you choose, you can have some wonderful toppings for your steak like garlic whiskey au poivre, *foie gras,* or melted *fromage.* There are also other choices like duck and chicken and ahi tuna, but most rave about the steaks. Those who I've known to eat at the Ranch always have the same giddy look when asked about their dining experience. (See Chef Jonas Favela's recipe for **Cointreau-Cured Scottish Salmon on Johnnycakes** on p. 246.) This is also the place you want to belly up to the unbelievably classy bar for a Cognac or Armagnac, or perhaps you want a truly fine wine to sip. The Ranch is beautifully classic and deliciously hard to beat.

Redrock Canyon Grill, 9221 Lake Hefner Pkwy., Lakeside District, Oklahoma City, OK 73120; (405) 749-1995; redrockcanyongrill.ehsrg .com; Southwestern; $$$. Sit and dine overlooking beautiful Lake Hefner while trying some outstanding food at Redrock Canyon Grill. Group around the outdoor bar and fire pit with your friends, and on the weekend, listen to some great live music. Sit on their boardwalk-style deck and watch the sunset, which is celebrated with the ringing of a bell and the retracting of the shades around the inside porch. The stuffed poblano is my favorite appetizer, with its creamy chicken and cheese filling inside a spicy fried poblano with a black bean and corn relish. Redrock's menu is made up of homey gourmet meats and is always delicious. They are known for their famous Persimmon Hill meat loaf, made of ground tenderloin and pork. Sunday brunch is a little less pricey and a great experience on the weekends as well, with items like Melodie's Chicken Potpie, and their Famous Iron Skillet Cornbread.

Red's Southern Diner, 840 W. Danforth Rd., Edmond, OK 73003; (405) 509-2635; redssoutherndiner.com; Southern; $$. Enter into the twilight zone of a fried chicken diner, as you see lawnmower ceiling fans, and perhaps the largest revolving chicken bucket in the world. Dine inside a vintage silver camper trailer and enjoy some great home-style cuisine. There is no menu at Red's, just a lit marquee sign on the wall displaying your choice of meats. Pick from chicken-fried steak, meat loaf, chicken potpie, and a variety of other meats and then gasp as the giant platter arrives in front of you. Sides are in large bowls to share and consist of mashed potatoes and cream gravy, creamed corn, salad, fried okra, and delicious Southern-style biscuits. Its kid-friendly atmosphere and home-style cooking make Red's Southern Diner a family favorite.

Saturn Grill, 6432 Avondale Dr., NW Oklahoma City, Oklahoma City, OK 73116; (405) 843-7114; saturngrill.com; Farm to Table; $.

From the flames seeming to lap at the walls to the funky hanging lights, this eatery makes you feel a little spunky and hip just upon entering. Chef-Owner Joseph Royer trained under two great Oklahoma City chef legends Kurt Fleischfresser from the Coach House and Alain Buthion from La Baguette, and then branched out on his own to create Saturn Grill, a fast-food meets gourmet restaurant with some truly wonderful cuisine. Order up a pizza, salad, or sandwich but what's exciting are the ingredients offered like seared salmon or Caribbean chicken to go on them. Check their website for seasonal specials for each day of the week like Indian mulligatawny soup. There is a second location at 4401 W. Memorial Rd., Oklahoma City, OK 73134; (405) 463-5594.

S&B Burger Joint, 5929 N. May Ave., NW Oklahoma City, Oklahoma City, OK; (405) 843-8777; sandbburgersokc.com; Burgers; $. S is for Shannon Roper, B is for Brian Neel, and first-time diners always come walking out of S&B Burger Joint with a new idea about burgers and fries. The menu full of eclectic burgers (to match the decor) and wine and beer pairings to go with each burger are already a bit of a change, but add in things like the Elvis Burger with peanut butter and bacon and Thanksgiving Fries—sweet potato fries with marshmallow crème, pecans, and cranberries—and this joint will keep your imagination and your taste buds spinning. Order the burger or scale it down so you can try two or three by asking for the slider versions. If that isn't enough, the pies are amazing! They are changed daily, and you will swoon over these treats. They also have a new location at 20 NW 9th St., Oklahoma City, OK 73102; (405) 843-8777.

Sean Cummings Irish Restaurant and Pub, 7523 N. May Ave., Nichols Hills/Lakeside, Oklahoma City, OK 73116; (405) 755-2622; Pub Food; $$. Chef Sean Cummings knows his Irish food. Just in case you don't, the Traditional menu lets you in on the lowdown on Irish terms like bangers (pork sausage) and black and white pudding (blood sausage and beef sausage), or you can opt for the Pub Fare menu of sandwiches and soups like Irish Fish Stew. Don't miss out on the fish and chips, which are served in a wire basket; they come out piping hot and the batter is delicious! Whichever route you decide to take, you're guaranteed to get something delicious and eat it in an authentic "pub" type atmosphere. On the weekends, visit the pub area for some great live Irish music and enjoy some down-home Irish beer and hard cider while rocking out.

The Shack Seafood and Oyster Bar, 303 NW 62nd St., NW Oklahoma City, Oklahoma City, OK 73118; (405) 608-4333; theshackok.com; Cajun/Creole; $$. The Shack Seafood and Oyster Bar is like a cross between a grass hut and a beachfront dive; the Cajun food is wonderful, which makes it a challenge for the staff to keep up with the throngs of people waiting to get in for lunch and dinner. Ask for the Oyster Brent appetizer (named after Brent Hickma, the owner), which is wildly popular among the locals. The oysters come out topped with generous portions of lump crab meat, shrimp, garlic butter and parmesan cheese. Or perhaps start off with the Shack's heavenly crab bisque. The Shack has their food shipped up twice a week fresh from Houston and you'll see all sorts of delectable dishes like crawfish, two kinds of gumbo, and my favorite, the seafood court bouillon with rice. You'll also hear some great bands live at the Shack; visit their Facebook page for a schedule of events.

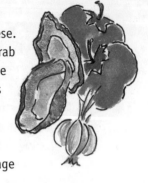

Signature Grill, 1317 E. Danforth Rd., Edmond, OK 73034; (405) 330-4548; signaturegrilledmond.com; Seafood/Steaks; $$$$. Chef Clay Falkner and his wife, Jessica, own the recently opened Signature Grill and it has already become a diamond in the rough in Edmond for food lovers. Chef Clay loves to put classic but innovative twists on food but keep it simple and delicious. He succeeds at every point. The food is fresh and high quality, the atmosphere is romantic and intimate, and the wine list has some rare and special offerings. Try the pan-seared Chilean sea bass with a roasted tomato butter sauce, and each entree is accompanied by your choice of two sides, each superbly delicious in its own right, like the green beans with chorizo and tomatoes. Make sure you call ahead for reservations, as space is limited and cozy.

The Sushi Bar, 1201 NW 178th St. #123, Edmond, OK 73012; (405) 285-7317; Sushi/Japanese; $$$. Beautiful modern Asian decor, intimate lounge areas with cozy couches and plasma televisions, and really good sushi make this place the best of both worlds. I mean, this is one classy sushi place, folks! Joyce and Jamison Han originally started this large restaurant on a much smaller scale, built up their clientele, and then gave us this lovely place a few years later. They must be doing something right! Try their ever-popular Captain Crunch Roll, which is a cooked roll with tempura crispy shrimp, crabstick, sliced cucumber, and avocado. The roll is then coated in crunchy tempura flakes and drizzled with a sweet and savory eel sauce. The dish is amazing, but just because the eatery is called The Sushi Bar doesn't mean they don't offer plenty of other temptations. For lunch, they have a reasonably priced bento box with various meat offerings. For dinner, start out with the Hamachi Kama, tender grilled yellowtail cheekbone with sea-salt soy glaze. There is also the kitchen menu with dinner items like steak or seafood entrees, or you can venture into duck or lamb as well, all cooked up with an Asian flair.

Tana Thai Bistro, 10700 N. May Ave., NW Oklahoma City, Oklahoma City, OK 73120; (405) 749-5590; Thai; $$. Thai cuisine is my favorite so I am a pretty finicky soul when searching out a Thai place. One of my few go-to places for Thai in Oklahoma City, Tana Thai Bistro has never disappointed. It's fresh and bright inside with added touches of class like stemware and real napkins. Don't be offended by the lady who commands the dining room; you'll grow to appreciate her and her suggestions. The curries are some of the best in town as is the classic pad thai, but venture away from the well-known Thai dishes and try the red snapper for something special, with its three-flavor sauce. Don't miss any of their soups as they are probably the best in town. Here's a little tip: Don't go past three on the spice recommendation unless your mouth is already numb! They season well at Tana Thai, and along with the heat comes some magnificent Thai flavor.

Tokyo Japanese Restaurant, 7516 N. Western Ave., Nichols Hills District, Oklahoma City, OK 73116; (405) 848-6733; tokyookc.com; Japanese/Sushi; $$. Ask most chefs or foodies where their favorite sushi place is in Oklahoma City, and you might be surprised. Not as fancy or modern as other places, Tokyo Japanese Restaurant remains a favorite among gastronomes, has true Japanese chefs, and is more reasonably priced than some of its competition. For a steal, create your own lunch by picking items from two lists, with miso soup, steamed rice, and a gyoza and shumai included, or try out one of their other menu items like tempura or *katsu* (fried cutlet of pork or chicken). For dinner order the Omakase Boat for two to three people. Your sushi will be served in an actual Asian-style wooden boat and you will receive a variety of sashimi slices, and a variety of rolls as well. The ultimate order at Tokyo Japanese, however, is the 100-piece sushi dinner meant for a table of six to eight hungry customers. Coming in at $100, this masterpiece won't leave you wanting.

West, 6714 N. Western Ave., Nichols Hills District, Oklahoma City, OK 73116; (405) 607-4072; westbar.com; Steaks/Seafood; $$$. Brothers David and Rick Haynes of Johnnie's Charcoal Broiler fame bring a sexy and upscale Southwest flair to West. In addition to addictive zucchini chips, West has a large variety of food, from great steak to vegetarian and gluten-free options. Try their prime beef tenderloin fixed five different ways, ranging from a grilled filet to beef and enchiladas. From fresh cucumber martinis to the Haynes Family Lemonade, check out the West Bar, which in addition to some fine wines, sports local and imported beer on tap or in bottles. West serves a great brunch on Saturday and Sunday from 10 a.m. to 4 p.m. with dishes like chicken-fried beef tenderloin. And check out their after-hours menu of burgers and late-night munchies as well.

Zarates Latin Mexican Grill, 706 S. Broadway Ave., Edmond, OK 73034; (405) 330-6400; zarateslatingrill.com; Latin American/ Peruvian; $$. Oklahoma City has its fair share of Peruvian residents and as a result a few tasty restaurants have been cropping up over the years. Once limited by the ingredients he had access to, Peruvian native Jorge Zarate first stuck with the typical Tex-Mex fare, but as the ability to get his home staples improved, his menu has slowly become more Peruvian. Part Caribbean and part Peruvian, you will find dishes like Jamaican jerk chicken or *lomito saltado*. You'll see things like plantains, yucca fries, and Honduran Banana Leaf Tamales. There is something truly unique about tamales prepared Peruvian-style; the masa is scrumptious and you will enjoy every bite.

Zorba's Mediterranean Cuisine, 6014 N. May Ave., NW Oklahoma City, Oklahoma City, OK 73112; (405) 947-7788; zorbasokc .com; Mediterranean/Greek; $$. Once a minuscule dive that we all loved and frequented, Zorba's went a bit more upscale in the past few years but still serves fine food. They truly have some of the best Greek food in the city and are a preference of most foodies. Every Friday and Saturday night, you can truly experience the culture by watching the belly dancers perform while you dine on such dishes as mousssaka, with its generous layers of eggplant, seasoned ground lamb, potato, cheese, wine, and breadcrumbs, or for the vegetarians, the lentil stew. Their dolma is also tender and seasoned to perfection. If you're craving Greek food, make sure you visit Zorba's.

Landmarks

The Coach House, 6437 Avondale Dr., Nichols Hills District, Oklahoma City, OK 73116; (405) 842-1000; thecoachhouseokc.com; Steaks/Seafood; $$$$. Resembling a fine country inn in Europe, the Coach House makes its fortunate diners feel incomparably special.This Oklahoma City landmark is under the careful watch of Chef-Owner Kurt Fleischfresser, perhaps the most celebrated chef in all of Oklahoma. The Coach House has also played host to guest chefs from time to time, including Jacques Pépin, Roland Passot, Rick Bayless, Jean-Louis Palladin, Hubert Keller, Hugh Carpenter,

CHEF SPOTLIGHT: KURT FLEISCHFRESSER

Kurt Fleischfresser's accolades would require many pages to list. A lot of the respected chefs in Oklahoma have been under his tutelage at some point in their careers. After leaving college and driving cross-country in his Volkswagen Rabbit, Kurt embarked on a culinary journey that would cover being apprentice chef for Chef Bernard Cretier of Le Vichyssoise in Chicago and several other prestigious places of fine dining. He has cooked for President George H.W. Bush and has been invited to the world-renowned James Beard House in New York City as part of the Great Regional Chefs Program. Chef Fleischfresser is also a two-time finalist in the prestigious Culinary Gold Cup Competition. In 2009, L'Academie de Gastronomie Brillat-Savarin recognized him for his contributions in education in the culinary arts, because many Oklahoma City chefs have gone through his internship programs and now have restaurants of their own. He, Julia Child, Paul Prudhomme, and Alan Hongrom are the only four American chefs to receive the honor. For over 8 years, Kurt has been in partnership with Carl Milam and together they operate the Western Concepts Group, which boasts some splendid Oklahoma City restaurants including **Sushi Neko** (p. 46), Musashi's, Wills Cafe, Will Rogers Theater, and **The Lobby Cafe & Bar** (p. 36), and we the diners, are so blessed to have him.

Bernard Cretier, and Deborah Madison. Their menu features only the finest and the freshest of local fare prepared with classic French techniques, and therefore changes monthly. At The Coach House you will dine on such items as a seared foie gras, which is fabulous. The restaurant's Caesar salad is among the best in Oklahoma, and if offered that month, try the seared duck breast and confit with rouennaise sauce; the delicious sauce is made of red wine, bone marrow, and duck liver that have been pureed together. Their wine list has been singled out by *The Wine Spectator*. Consider yourself privileged if you are under Chef Kurt's care, for you will have a noteworthy meal you will never forget. (See Chef Kurt's recipe for **Grilled Catfish with a Sweet Potato Tamale** on p. 253.)

Coit's Root Beer Drive-In, 5001 N. Portland Ave., NW Oklahoma City, Oklahoma City, OK 73112; (405) 946-8778; Burgers/Breakfast $. One of my earliest memories of Oklahoma City eateries when I moved here over 20 years ago was visiting Coit's and tasting its homemade root beer for the first time. When dining inside, you get it in a frosted mug and just the thought of it still makes me smile. Coit's has been around since 1954, when hot rods flocked to the drive-in lanes to grab an icy mug and a hot dog or two, which are as legendary as their namesake beverage. There is a selection of seven dogs on the menu as well as hamburgers and even breakfast offerings. In the new world of gourmet, many may not think much of this fare, but to us in Oklahoma City, it is nostalgia at its finest. There are two additional locations at 2500 W. Western Ave.,

Oklahoma City, OK 73109; (405) 632-6976 and another at 4101 N. Pennsylvania Ave., Oklahoma City, OK; (405) 524-0655.

The Haunted House, 7101 Miramar Blvd., NW Oklahoma City, Oklahoma City, OK 73111; (405) 478-1417; hauntedhouserestaurant .com; Steak House/Seafood; $$$. Back in the 1960s, an automobile dealer was shot, and shortly afterward his stepdaughter was accused of the murder. What followed was a tragic chain of events that led to the estate being sold and re-opened as a landmark restaurant of fine dining, which has brought diners and intrigue to the eatery ever since. Believe it or not, this mansion was renovated into a fine-dining establishment, only open for dinner, and has become a legend of sorts for young bucks proposing to their honeys or visiting celebrities. The menu is of the classic, old-school steak and seafood variety.

Junior's, 2601 NW Expy., NW Oklahoma City, Oklahoma City, OK 73112; (405) 848-5597; juniorsokc.com; Steak House; $$$. Located on the ground floor of the west Oil Center building, Junior's has been here for us since 1973 and we appreciate that. It's nice to know some things never change, like their real full-service bar and their tableside Caesar salad, made with real anchovies, garlic, and egg yolks. The decor has been the same it seems, as well, with its red velveteen chairs, glass-partitioned private dining tables for two, and the bar. Enjoy the piano bar nightly starting at 8:30 and be there for Anita White on the weekend. The steaks are quality Angus beef and the service is impeccable.

La Baguette Bistro, 7408 N. May Ave., NW Oklahoma City, Oklahoma City, OK 73116; (405) 562-5139; labaguettebistro.com; French/Bakery; $$$. Brothers Michel and Alain Buthion have become synonymous with outstanding cuisine in Oklahoma City. Michel heads up the business side and Chef Alain is the genius behind the delicious food at any of their restaurants. Putting down roots in Oklahoma since the late '80s, these French natives have pleased us with the best of both worlds, blending together French and American cuisine into deliciousness. Chef Alain trained in Grenoble, France, and continues to return each year to France for inspiration. This is your place to go for *foie gras* or beef tartare, and a good *croque madame,* but everything here is amazingly good from the *fromage* to the burgers. (See Chef Alain's recipe for **Goat Cheese Cake with Prosciutto, Local Honey & Arugula with Lemon Vinaigrette** on p. 244.) If you've ever had a French-made omelet, you know how scrumptiously perfect it can be. Visit their *boucherie,* bakery, and deli next door for a special treat! Bon appétit!

Michael's Grill, 2824 W. Country Club Dr., NW Oklahoma City, Oklahoma City, OK 73116; (405) 810-9000; michaelsgrillokc.com; Steak House/Seafood; $$$$. I absolutely love places like Michael's Grill: old-fashioned, elegant steak houses that make you feel like a king or queen or . . . a member of the Mafia. No, Michael's is not a scary place, but hey, the mafiosos always ate at the coolest places, didn't they? First off it would be criminal to not get the Caesar salad at Michael's Grill, as the chef, Michael Sills, has been making it tableside and from scratch here and at his previous restaurant **Junior's** (p. 85) for many years. But before you do that, start off with the shrimp and lobster stuffed rellenos. I am known to love poblano peppers, but stuffed with shrimp, lobster, and three cheeses, along with onions, cilantro, and jalapeños? Fabulous! And just try not to swoon over the mussel appetizer. The broth is heaven and you'll want to sop it up with hunks of the complimentary Italian bread. Try Michael's favorite steak, the 13-ounce K.C. Strip, a buttery tender grilled sensation you'll want to savor, one slow bite at a time. For dessert have a rich, velvety slice of chocolate gateau. Say hi to Michael, as you'll most likely see him. He loves to visit with his customers, a sure sign the man loves what he does. And so do we.

Specialty Stores, Markets & Producers

The Children's Center Farmers' Market, 6800 NW 39th Expy.; NW Oklahoma City, Bethany, OK 73008; (405) 789-6711. This small but quaint farmers' market is located on the front lawn of the Bethany Children's Center and is open Memorial Day weekend through Labor Day weekend on Thurs 4 p.m. to 7:30 p.m. and Sat 8 a.m. to 1 p.m. It offers up a variety of sustainably produced local foods including vegetables, herbs, locally produced honey, and fresh-baked bread.

Culinary Kitchen, 7302 N. Western Ave., NW Oklahoma City, Oklahoma City, OK 73116; (405) 418-4884. This store has a great selection of kitchen products for all your high end kitchen needs. Owner Russ Johnson offers up an inventory of high-performance appliances, kitchen gadgets, and the best cutting boards and knives. You'll also find specialty items like beautiful wine decanters, herb pots, and a bevy of food items like spreads and other gourmet offerings. On Saturday Russ conducts cooking demonstrations where he puts some of Culinary Kitchen's appliances to good use.

Epicurean's Pantry, 1333 N. Santa Fe Ave., Edmond, OK 73003; (405) 471-5777. There is a reason Leah Haskins uses the word "Epicurean" in the name of her store. "Epicurean" means to be devoted to the pursuit of sensual pleasure, especially to the enjoyment of good food and comfort. Browse through the shelves packed full of gourmet delights, like her Cocktail Corner with all sorts of fun stuff to make drinks at home. Gaze at imported California olive oils and aged balsamic vinegars. There is even a meat case with local fresh meats to purchase as well as some magnificent selections of cheese. Make sure you allot plenty of time to shop at Epicurean's Pantry. You'll love what you see and want to savor it one slow step at a time.

Ferria Latina Market, 4909 NW 23rd St., NW Oklahoma City, Oklahoma City, OK 73127; (405) 606-4004. Looking for special cooking ingredients from Mexico and Central or South America? Ferria Latina Market probably has them. Featuring produce and canned, jarred, and frozen foods from Costa Rica, Brazil, Colombia, Venezuela, Honduras, Nicaragua and Peru, this Latino market offers all sorts of fun stuff.

The Festival Market Place Farmers' Market in Edmond, 2733 Marilyn Williams Dr., Edmond, OK 73034; (405) 359-4630. Just west of Broadway in downtown Edmond, the Festival Market Place is on 1st Street and has its own  roofed outdoor structure to house it each week. Open from 8 a.m. to 1 p.m. Wed and Sat, the Edmond Farmers' Market has plenty of fruits, vegetables, meats, eggs, local wine, flowers, pastries, and more, and is my favorite place to go on Saturday. Families pushing strollers come out to buy produce and fresh herbs and there are even a few food trucks set up that offer barbecue, lunch items, and shaved ice treats for the kids. All food must be labeled if it's local or not.

Green Goodies by Tiffany, 5840 N. Classen Curve, Nichols Hills District, Oklahoma City, OK 73118; (405) 842-2288; green goodiesokc.com. Another cupcake place, right? Not so with Green Goodies by Tiffany. Owner Tiffany Magness offers some of the most

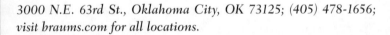

HOME-GROWN CHAINS: BRAUM'S ICE CREAM AND DAIRY

I have many fond memories of taking my kids to Braum's after a hot summer night ballgame. Braum's is a local dairy that has grown into a chain that you can find on just about every corner in Oklahoma City. Founders Bill and Mary Braum started up their dairy in 1933 and the stores have now been transformed into mini-markets where customers can opt to buy fresh sweet milk and delicious ice cream along with many other grocery items. I am hopelessly in love with the Peanut Butter Cup Sundae and Braum's Cappuccino Chunky Chocolate frozen yogurt.

3000 N.E. 63rd St., Oklahoma City, OK 73125; (405) 478-1656; visit braums.com for all locations.

delicious varieties of organic, vegan, gluten-free, and peanut-free cupcakes you'll ever put in your mouth. Also, soy-free and sugar-free varieties are available by special order. Served on environmentally friendly paperware, this whole place is green . . . just as its name says.

La Baguette La Boucherie, 7408 N. May Ave., NW Oklahoma City, Oklahoma City, OK 73116; (405) 840-3407; labaguettebistro .com/butcher. Need a free-range chicken, whole pheasant, duck, or rabbit? La Baguette is the place to go. Adjacent to its wonderful bistro, La Boucherie has delightful offerings like *foie gras, fromage,* and lovely French baguettes. The butchers here are experts and they know about everything, from wine pairings to how to cook the meat you buy. Browse their freezer and cooled section for duck confit, racks of lamb, or premade items like Dave's meat loaf, homemade sausage or stuffed large vegetables. I love this place because a perfect French pâté is always on hand.

The Meat House OKC, 2249 W. Danforth Rd., Edmond, OK 73083; (405) 509-2900. An endless plethora of delicious meat, cheeses, and other wonderful goodies await your pleasure at The Meat House. Like an old-fashioned neighborhood butcher meets modern gourmet market, this place has mouthwatering cuts, and the staff is very knowledgeable in helping you understand how to prepare and cook them as well. Pre-marinated meats, homemade sausage, rolled and stuffed meats, Boar's Head meats and cheeses, fresh local produce, homemade pasta, and countless other items await your every need at The Meat House. They also have in-house chefs who prepare and box up dinner items for you to grab and take home for a meal.

Raspberries N Crème, 2925 Lakeside Cir., NW Oklahoma City, Oklahoma City, OK, 73120; (405) 755-3560; raspberriesncreme.com. Ask any locals about a Raspberries N Crème cake, and they'll sigh in delight. And usually they'll mention the ribbon cake, a sinful concoction of layers of chocolate cake, moist sour cream white cake, fresh Italian cream, and strawberries in between, fresh whipped cream, and adorned across the top with fresh flowers. And that's just one of their delicious confections at this OKC sweet staple.

Spices of India Market, 3647 NW 39th St., NW Oklahoma City, Oklahoma City, OK 73112; (405) 942-7813. Find everything you need to make your favorite Indian dishes here at Spices of India Market. From Indian sodas to paneer, you will be transported to another land while browsing the aisles. Find whole cardamom pods, cinnamon sticks, and Taj Mahal tea to make chai at home or buy a variety of lentils in every color of the rainbow. Check the freezer case for unique items like green almonds, or the refrigerator case for dates and figs. They also have a kitchen section for cooking utensils used in Indian cooking, like a press to make fresh naan. Toward the front of the store, you will see beautiful Indian clothing for sale and tucked away in the back corner is a little counter where a few days of the week, you can smell food cooked up and sold at the counter.

Sweet Cherry's Sugar Art Bakery, 5116 N. MacArthur Blvd., NW Oklahoma City, Warr Acres, OK 73122; (405) 720-2253; sweetcherrys bakery.com. Visit this little gem of a bakery to find some wonderful cupcakes, cookies, and baked goods in their glass case, and all are made with whole eggs and the finest ingredients. They also make fabulous cakes for weddings and other events, but what I truly love is stopping by to buy things for my home baking needs. There are unique cookie cutters, piping tips in various sizes and styles, regular and disposable piping bags, fondant, colored sugars and sprinkles, and boxes to package your homemade treats, along with a variety of other bakery items. Want to learn how to decorate cakes? Sweet Cherry's offers classes. Check out their website for details.

Sweete Memories Bakery, 6501 N. May Avenue, NW Oklahoma City, Oklahoma City, OK 73116; (405) 842-4799; sweete memories.com. Renowned for its delectable custom cakes, Sweete Memories also makes my most favorite iced sugar cookies on the planet. Order a custom cake, brownies, pie, cheese cake, chocolate-dipped strawberries or many other treats, or just stop in and grab something out of their daily selection of "grab and go" offerings like mini-loaf pumpkin and banana bread, petits fours, lemon bars (scrumptious!), or the cookies—make sure you try the iced sugar cookies!

T, an Urban Teahouse, 7518 N. May Ave., NW Oklahoma City, Oklahoma City, OK 73116; (405) 418-4333; urban-teahouse.com. Airy with punches of brightly colored furniture, local artist canvases on the wall, and definitely more of an urban feel than a frilly tea room, T, an Urban Teahouse offers a wide variety of loose-leaf tea brewed correctly and local baked goods from Prairie Thunder Baking Company. Choose an individual pot or a pot for two and sit and sip it while snacking on chocolates from Dude, Sweet as well. Once a month, T's owner, Christy Jennings, changes out the local artist wall decor and celebrates with a tea cocktail reception. T also offers a selection of super-cute tea ware for purchase along the walls of the store.

Vintage Timeless Coffee, 900 NW 150th St., Oklahoma City, OK 73013; (405) 752-0038; facebook.com/VintageCoffeeOK. This local java joint offers up some really good brew like espresso, lattes, French press, and chai. Visit them in the morning for some great breakfast sandwiches or at lunch try one of the specials of the day like the Santa Fe chicken sandwich. The cinnamon knot under the Vintage Favorites is outstanding, and they always have *kolaches* available that are brought in from **Kolache Kitchen** (p. 69).

Learn to Cook

Cooking Girl, 8020A N. May Ave., NW Oklahoma City, Oklahoma City, OK 73120; (405) 607-1187; cookinggirl.org/general/cooking-classes. Chef Christa Carretero attended the California Culinary Academy and ate her way through San Francisco while doing so. Oh yes, and while she was there, she interned at Chez Panisse and Ponzu. After she graduated, she hit Washington, DC, and worked with Chef Jose Andres at the Think Food Group, and also with her mentor Katsuya Fukushima at Cafe Atlantico and Minibar. She headed here to open her own business of catering and cooking classes. You can check out her website for current classes on offer. There are nine customized kitchens with over 31,000 square feet!

Francis Tuttle School of Culinary Arts, 12777 N. Rockwell Ave., NW Oklahoma City, OK 73142; (405) 717-7799; francistuttle.edu/culinaryarts. Francis Tuttle has offered culinary classes before, but space was limited as was class size. Recently, they've expanded by building an entire new massive wing onto the school that will provide a state-of-the-art culinary school the likes of which our state (and most states) have not seen. From a room that is temperature controlled with marble countertops for making chocolate to a charcuterie and curing room to a pastry kitchen, all the kitchens are equipped with the finest equipment possible. Students can learn to butcher meat and fish in the butchering kitchen. Students will be able to obtain real-life experience with their cuisine by doing internships and externships at the school, including the restaurant, bakery, or cafeteria. This is a world-class learning environment and to go along with that there is a chef demonstration kitchen just to bring in the best of the best for the students. From the outdoor kitchen at the restaurant patio to the wood-burning brick pizza oven, we expect this facility to turn out some future stars here in Oklahoma! High school students have the option to enroll for free as a part of their education, or anyone else

CHEF SPOTLIGHT: MARC DUNHAM, DIRECTOR OF CULINARY ARTS AT FRANCIS TUTTLE TECHNOLOGY CENTER

Marc Dunham has a strong and diverse culinary background, which allows him to show great versatility. His talents extend beyond the kitchen to include food science and nutrition, writing, project development, television, and Internet. Marc's passion is food, education, and operating successful businesses. Marc is currently the creator, writer, and host of *Oklahoma Cooks,* which airs on KSBI 52 in Oklahoma as well as serving as director of the prestigious Francis Tuttle Technology Center, currently in development in northwest Oklahoma City.

Marc completed an A.O.S. from the Culinary Institute of America and a B.S. degree in Nutrition and Foods from Texas State University, and has cooked in a variety of kitchens from New York to Austin and now Oklahoma City.

Marc's hard work and talent led him to the James Beard House on July 15, 2010, where he was the featured chef. Marc believes in utilizing local and seasonal products and precise techniques to create food that is delicious, bold, and unique. He mixes his German/Hispanic Texas roots with his work and education experiences from New York City to create a unique blend of Latin-influenced cuisine.

can enroll in the program as well. Visit the website for details. (See Chef Marc Dunham's recipe for **Braised Beef Tongue & Veal Cheek** on p. 249.)

Kam's Kookery and Guilford Gardens, 2834 Guilford Ln., Lakeside District, Oklahoma City, OK 73120; (405) 840-0725, kams kookery.com. Kamala Gamble, chef, gardener, and cooking instructor, is located in suburban NW Oklahoma City where she owns a 2-acre spread of urban farming that is all organic and lovely. Pretty much year-round, CSA bags are available from her garden and when they are offered, she also offers cooking classes using her own produce (check website to see if they are available). You get to sit around her kitchen table and watch while she cooks up a themed night of wonder.

South Oklahoma City, Capitol Hill District, Moore & Norman

The Southern end of Oklahoma City, which merges into Moore and then Norman, is a diverse but delectable part of the city and its surrounding areas as well. From the food truck scene on SW 29th Street to Korean food in Moore to the four blocks of Campus Corner around the University of Oklahoma in Norman, you'll find some fabulous places to dine in these areas.

Bella Vista Italian Kitchen, 5801 S. Western Ave. W, South Oklahoma City, Oklahoma City, OK 73109; (405) 631-1717; Italian; $. Dina and Milt Korkolis are Greek and serve a few Greek dishes at this diamond-in-the-rough eatery. Both the Greek menu and the larger Italian menu are old-school classic and wonderful. Large portions and wonderfully fresh ingredients will leave you more than satisfied and smiling with pleasure. For starters, try the spanakopitakia with its delicate and flaky crust; and for a meal, truly there is not much you can go wrong with, but the lasagna is heavenly. The specialty is the calzones; they're the size of your head and filled with a homemade sauce, cheese, and your choice of meat. Make sure you ask for to-go boxes—if you have a very large appetite, it will be filled at Bella Vista, and then some.

Benvenuti's Ristorante, 105 W. Main St., Norman, OK 73069; (405) 310-5271; benvenutisristorante.com; Italian; $$$. Executive Chef Anthony Compagni started out cooking as a young teenager and then headed off to the Scottsdale Culinary Institute Le Cordon Bleu, where he graduated with honors. At Benvenuti's, Chef Compagni offers up a truly unique seasonal menu using the freshest, finest, and most natural ingredients he can find. You'll get wonderful dishes like wild sturgeon, braised cannellini beans, and roasted tomatoes, or Pig and Scallops, with scallops and braised pork belly. Pick anything off of their *primi piatti* menu (first courses) and sip on a heady wine to go with it from their lovely wine list, including three fine Italian reds. Do not miss their truffle fries—I cannot stress this point enough. Finish the evening off with one of their desserts; I have no idea how to pick just one but I'd go with the Il Gatto, a chocolate mousse creation chock-full of delicious surprises.

Cafe Plaid, 333 W. Boyd St., Norman, OK 73069; (405) 360-2233; cafeplaid.com; Sandwiches/Soups; $. Live music, great food, and an excellent patio make this small college town cafe a favorite among local diners. Want a good espresso? Enjoy a welcoming atmosphere and setting? Like free Wi-Fi? This is the place. Sandwiches use quality ingredients like Boar's Head deli meats, sun-dried tomato pesto, grilled veggies and homemade focaccia bread. The soups are hearty and fabulous. They offer some great combos like the Salad Sampler, where for under five bucks you can get a choice of three salads and a cookie. Portions are generous and combined with the atmosphere, this little college joint is pretty darn cool to dine at.

The Earth Natural Cafe & Deli, 746 Asp Ave., Norman, OK 73069; (405) 573-5933; Brunch/Deli; $. You can't help but feel just a bit more refreshed after eating at The Earth Natural Cafe & Deli. From the light wooden bar that overlooks the wall-mounted Organic Menu in front of it, to the helpful, welcoming staff, you

Home-Grown Chains: Coolgreens

Looking for a place that offers fresh, healthy ingredients where you can build your own sandwich, wrap, pizza, or salad? Coolgreens is your place. This quickly growing local chain has a wonderful menu of preconceived offerings, or you can go through the line and pick and create your own.

Their pizzas are a favorite of mine and are based on a whole-grain, nutty-type flatbread. My personal favorite is the Coolgreens Skinny; the toppings on this baby are basil pesto, arugula, figs, goat cheese, roasted grapes, sundried tomatoes, and walnuts. The combination of sweet and savory really knocks your socks off. Bit of a hummus fan? You'll love the hummus pizza with artichoke hearts, bean sprouts, carrots, feta, kalamata olives, sun-dried tomatoes, and lavishly spread with roasted garlic hummus.

They don't skimp on the salads either. The wild sockeye salmon salad is amazing as is the ahi tuna niçoise and the Plaza Skinny. Coolgreens makes all their salad dressings in house and you will see offerings like lime jalapeño vinaigrette and orange Catalina. Their homemade soups are fabulous as well. The wild mushroom and arugula and the red chicken pozole are definite keepers. The drinks at Coolgreens might be all natural and healthy, but that doesn't mean they're not delicious. They offer up beverages like Pellegrino, Izze sodas, and Honest Tea, as well as giant urns of water with lemons or cucumbers floating in them. For dessert don't leave without trying their frozen yogurt or sorbet creations in flavors like dark chocolate or coconut. Check out their website, coolgreens.com, for location information.

want to come back here again and again. This airy place pleases vegetarians and vegans alike and offers up organic fresh juice along with smoothies, coffee, and healthy teas like yerba maté. Want my advice? Get a scone to go with your beverage. They are fabulously fresh and vegan. The Earth serves breakfast, brunch, lunch, snacks, and supper. There is something for everyone here. The immensely popular Über Burger won't leave you missing the meat and there is a bevy of other things to try as well. Feeling sick? Try the Dragonslayer Shot: fresh squeezed lemon juice with garlic, ginger and . . . habañero! I can pretty much guarantee you'll walk out of The Earth feeling much better than when you walked in.

Fusion Cafe, 1224 N. Broadway St., Moore, OK 73160; (405) 799-4900; facebook.com/fusion.cafeok; Japanese/Korean; $. Stained concrete floors, soft yellow walls with black warehouse ceilings, and an inviting staff set the stage for this Korean Japanese mix of an eatery. Rev. John Chong brings some fabulous Korean hometown love to his dishes at Fusion Cafe. While the restaurant states it is a Korean Japanese fusion, the real stars are their *bulgogi* and perhaps the fusion comes with America's love of buffalo wings as they serve up some fantastic Asian chicken wings with your choice of several Asian-inspired sauces. There are also some fabulous items like teri-yaki bowls and bento "rice boxes" to try as well. Take a taste of the unlimited kimchee bar with Chong's version of this Korean staple and grab a soda out of the glass case.

The Garage Burgers and Beer, 307 E. Main St., Norman, OK 73069; (405) 701-7035; eatatthegarage.com; Burgers/Tacos; $. Tanner Smith and Brandon Kissler opened this "car bar" in Norman and gave it a new twist—that of a garage bar complete with road signs, yellow lines painted on the floor, and a whole lot of good burgers and beer. Though the menu mainly consists of stick-to-your-ribs diner fare, they offer twists on the classics, like a Spicy Sriracha Bleu Burger with grilled onions and jalapeños. With a burger, fries, and onion rings and some interesting dipping sauces (Special Sauce: 1000?), there are also some other fun choices like spicy or fish tacos. Burgers are offered with a choice of meat that includes ground Angus, ground turkey, garden, or buffalo. You can have them on a bun or wrapped in lettuce. Out on the town for some fun? The Garage also has Skee-Ball and arcade games and, of course, the latter part of the name . . . beer. They have it all at The Garage. There is a second location at 601 S. Bryant, Edmond, OK 73034; (405) 341-5801.

Grill on the Hill, 324 SW 25th St., Capitol Hill District, Oklahoma City, OK 73109; (405) 634-9866; Burgers; $. You must love a place that has something on the menu called Atomic Tots, right? Up on Capitol Hill, Rory and Norma serve up breakfast and lunch every day except Friday, when they serve up breakfast, lunch, and dinner! Their no-fuss menu offers burgers, fries, breakfast burritos, and some surprises like a meat loaf breakfast sandwich and an Indian taco burger, served open faced and covered in homemade beans, chili, lettuce, salsa, cheddar, tomato, and diced onions. Pay attention to the daily specials as they are always popular and have diners abuzz. They also have good old-fashioned diner-type fare with chicken-fried steak and the like, and it's all down-home, good cooking with large portions that will satisfy a healthy appetite. And don't leave without trying some of their mouthwatering pies or cinnamon apple fritters.

Local, 2262 W. Main St., Norman, OK 73069; (405) 928-5600; eatatlocal.com; Farm to Table; $$. What do three sisters and a great local chef have in common? They can all be found at Local, a newly opened eatery located in Norman. Melissa Scaramucci, Heather Steele, and Abby Clark have brought us a real treat of an eatery with the help of Chef Ryan Parrott. Their ever-changing menu is based on local, seasonal ingredients. They source produce, meat, and dairy from Oklahoma farms to bring diners delicious dishes like Green Chile Chowder, a tasty bowl of roasted corn, potatoes, green chiles, and a corn-jalapeño madeline. Try their daily raviolis, which are pillows of goodness filled with different ingredients each day, like spicy smoked beef and corn. Visit on Sunday for Local's family-style brunch with house-smoked and cured maple bacon. See Chef Parrott's recipe for **Moroccan Lamb with Tomato Jam** on p. 260.

The Mediterranean Grill, 7868 S. Western Ave., South Oklahoma City, Oklahoma City, OK 73139; (405) 601-8959; themedgrill.com; Mediterranean; $$. Co-owners Andy Stagle and Fred Foroozan

CHEF SPOTLIGHT: RYAN PARROTT

Ryan Parrott has had a passion for cooking dating back to his teenage years. When he was just 19, Ryan was given the kitchen manager position at Tommy's Italian. This set him on the track to eventually conceiving the now-closed Vineyard in Edmond. Ryan went on to work in other local restaurants such as Petroleum Club, Switzer's Lighthouse, Boulevard Steakhouse, 501 Ranch Steakhouse, The Mantel Wine Bar and Bistro, and Deep Fork Grill. Through it all, Ryan became a much loved chef in the Oklahoma City scene. His career took a different turn in 2008 when he partnered with Robert Painter and re-invented **Iguana Mexican Grill** (p. 130) and was instrumental in making it a beloved Oklahoma City eatery with a southwest flair. In March 2012, Ryan opened the doors of **Local** (p. 104), an eatery with a farm-to-fork philosophy where he continues to wow audiences with his delicious fare.

dreamed of one day opening a restaurant that would showcase fresh and exciting Middle Eastern cuisine, and in 2008 their dream came true. This brightly decorated Mediterranean spot features some wonderfully done things like authentic kebab skewers (Turkish style), made with choice cuts of beef and chicken that have been marinated in flavors from Iran, molded around sticks, and set over an open grill. Their falafel is delicious, and the gyros sport a delicious *tzatziki* that is made with house-made yogurt. Check them out daily for their hot stews of the day with a Middle Eastern flair. You can order a beer or a nice glass of wine at The Mediterranean Grill, so stop in soon and see why this little place is quickly becoming a destination for some of the best gyros in town.

Michelangelo's Coffee and Wine Bar, 207 E Main St., Norman, OK 73069; (405) 579-3387; michelangeloscoffeeandwine.com; Coffee/Dessert/Wine; $. Where can you go to get a great glass of port? Where in Norman do I recommend for a café au lait? How about a nice slice of homemade cake or a good breakfast sandwich or a gourmet cheese plate? The answer to all of the above questions is Michelangelo's Coffee and Wine Bar. From their panini lunch menu to gourmet pizzas, Michelangelo's is a quaint and artsy place complete with live music. Michael Palermo and his wife Paula have brought something special to Norman. Choose a lovely bottle of wine off their distinctive wine list (by the bottle and glass) and relax with a piece of delectable chocolate from their candy selection. The atmosphere is cozy and warm and friendly. You'll feel right at home at Michelangelo's.

O Asian Fusion, 105 12th Ave. SE, Norman, OK 73071; oasian fusion.com; Asian Fusion/Sushi; $$. Attapol "Nui" Chuntarasoun came from Thailand to the University of Oklahoma as a student in the late '90s and opened his own restaurant, but now has teamed up to chef for Stephanie and Dirk O'Hara and Ziayien Hwang (from Taiwan, and a former professor from O.U.) and developed a fun

Asian-fused menu for them. You will find dishes from Thailand, but also some pretty good sushi and Korean items. The inside of O is always packed with people waiting to get in and the ambience is really cool, from the cascading waterfall glass partition down the center of the room with an "O" as its centerpiece to the throw pillows lining the seats against the wall. Sit at the sushi bar and watch the sushi chefs at work and sip on warm or chilled sake off their extensive sake menu. One of their signature rolls, the Heaven Roll is still one of my all-time favorite sushi creations with coconut shrimp, asparagus, crab, and topped with thinly sliced lemon, seven spices, and garlic mayo.

Panang, 9022 S. Pennsylvania Ave., South Oklahoma City, Oklahoma City, OK 73159; (405) 691-9989; Thai; $$. From the warm wood-paneled walls to the quality ingredients that go into their Thai inspired dishes, you'll know why folks are driving out of their way to visit this eatery in the southern end of town. Their curries are praised far and wide across the city and their *tom yum* soup is the best I believe I've ever had. It comes served in a large silver bowl similar to a bundt pan and is swimming with all sorts of vegetables in a rich broth. The lunch special is not for the faint of heart—it changes daily, and each special offers a spring roll, rice or pad thai, curry, and a stir fry. And the kicker? It's less than $10 and you'll go away more than full, without a disappointment.

Home-Grown Chains: Earl's Rib Palace

With six locations all in Oklahoma City and Edmond, Earl's (earlsribpalace.com) has been pleasing us with their fantastic barbecue for almost 20 years. Here is how it works at Earl's: Go in and get your drink first, then get in line and order. The husband is a huge fan of the Smokestack Sandwich, which offers chopped brisket and a hot link sliced in half and stacked on the sandwich, which is then topped with creamy coleslaw. I prefer the ribs, chopped brisket, or smoked turkey breast dinner with some of Earl's famous sides, like their baked beans or fried okra. The thing I get most excited about, and have for years, is the blackberry cobbler. Served up in a large bowl, it is topped with three scoops of vanilla ice cream and sprinkled with cinnamon sugar. It's sinful and absolutely delicious.

Pepe Delgado's, 702 Asp Ave., Norman, OK 73069; (405) 321-6232; Mexican; $. Emilio Salinas, who learned his way around a kitchen in Mexico and California, brings a healthy option to Mexican cooking at Pepe Delgado's. First off, try one (or all) of their four freshly made salsas with avocado, tomatillo, and a fiery habañero version. For entree choices, you'll find things like grilled fish and black beans without the extra fat—Pepe Delgado's likes to keep things healthy and they don't use animal fat of any kind. This place is a great refuge for vegetarians as every dish on the menu has a veggie equivalent as well. On Saturday they do a Mexican barbecue of slow-cooked beef that is wildly popular and their Enchiladas Oaxacas with their savory mole sauce are absolutely delicious. Sip on some *agua de Jamaica,* a hibiscus tea, or a *horchata* with its creamy cinnamon vanilla goodness. Pepe's also has a nice alfresco patio for dining in nice weather!

Pickerman's Soup & Sandwiches, 8916 S. Pennsylvania Ave., South Oklahoma City, Oklahoma City, OK 73159; (405) 685-0000; Sandwiches; $. There are a few things that make a good sandwich shop. Fresh bread tops the list and you will find it at Pickerman's. Friendly staff is another and the folks who own Pickerman's make sure they greet you with a smile and they'll chat with you as well. This is the type of family-friendly place that earns its loyal customers through positive word of mouth. Try the Numerio Uno sandwich with its scrumptious drizzle of Italian dressing. If you're craving a quick sandwich or bowl of soup on the run and are in the neighborhood, Pickerman's is a good choice.

Royal Bavaria Brewery, 3401 S. Sooner Rd., Moore, OK 73165; (405) 799-7666; royal-bavaria.com; Brewpub/German; $$$. Executive chef, owner, and native German Andy Gmeiner attended culinary school in Munich before he was hired by Jog Kuhne, a Munich-based businessman and the original owner here, to be the chef at Royal Bavaria Brewery, which brought him overseas to Oklahoma. Eventually in 2008 he bought the restaurant and made it his own. He prides himself on making all his German creations from scratch and the beer is brewed in house in the giant brew vats you'll see upon arriving. The eatery was designed to resemble a Bavarian farmhouse; there is an outdoor beer garden in the warmer months where you can enjoy one of the house brews that are brewed within the guidelines of the German Purity Law (you can also take home a keg with you). Try the *Kartoffelsuppe mit Würstchen* for starters (potato soup with bacon, a mix of vegetables, and sausage slices) and then move on to the house favorite, the Wiener schnitzel, crispy brown and sautéed in butter.

Sergio's Italian Bistro, 104 E. Gray St., Norman, OK 73069; (405) 573-7707; sergiositalianbistro.vpweb.com; Italian; $$. This reasonably priced, family-friendly Italian place in Norman serves large, fresh, and homemade portions of delicious Italian cuisine, like their wonderful gnocchi. From the homemade focaccia bread that serves as the base for their roasted sandwiches to the simple

choices of pasta and sauce, this eatery is always busy with hungry customers. Their spaghetti alla carbonara is delicious in its sauce of egg, Parmesan cheese, and bacon butter and comes in at a mere $7.50. They also offer some fabulous salads for those wanting to avoid carbs. Their roasted vegetable salad uses seasonal vegetables and all their salads come with a choice of their homemade (there's that word again!) dressings.

The Stuffed Olive, 12215 S. Pennsylvania Ave., South Oklahoma City, Oklahoma City, OK 73170; (405) 735-7593; stuffedolivecafe .com; Sandwiches/Subs; $. Owner Andrea Durow opened this deliciously wonderful deli that offers decidedly fresh fare and dishes made from scratch. The inside is quaint and charming and at the Stuffed Olive, you will find menu items to layer on your sandwich with panache, like brie cheese, roasted Roma tomatoes, pesto mayo, and basil vinaigrette. These, along with some wonderful meats, make up one of the finest deli sandwiches you'll get from a local place here in Oklahoma City. Their soups are thick and rich, and the salads are drizzled with house-made dressings. A favorite among locals is the OMG Chicken Salad, served open-faced on a slice of focaccia complete with artichoke hearts, onion, olive salad, and a bounty of flavor.

Sweet Basil Thai Cuisine, 211 W. Main St., Norman, OK 73069; (405) 217-8424; Thai; $$. Located in old downtown Norman,

Sweet Basil is the best of both worlds if you're a Thai lover. It sports the ambience of a fine steak house combined with great Thai food. When you're at Sweet Basil, you're pretty much in curried Asian cuisine heaven. You'll see some not-so-typical Thai offerings on their menu, and all are delicious. This is the first place I ever sampled Jungle Curry, and the sauce is fabulously chock-full of shredded bok choy and other veggies. Most Thai places serve pad thai with rice noodles, but at Sweet Basil you can opt for egg noodles (*pad thai ba-mee*) or Singaporean noodles (*pad tha sen-mee*) or even with glass noodles or flat noodles. If you're around for Christmas, the restaurant is decorated beautifully with multiple trees and lights, which add to the ambience. For dessert, don't miss the sticky rice mango; it's fabulous!

Tarahumaras Mexican Cafe, 702 N. Porter Ave., Norman, OK 73071; (405) 360-8070; tarahumarasrestaurant.com; Mexican; $$. The brick building with the red trim and bright colors beckons one into Tarahumaras, the red-trimmed walls and guitar player walking around bid you to stay, and the food cinches it. Make sure and ask for the house salsa, a creamy blend of avocado and punchy peppers and cool it down with a margarita or something off their *bebidas* (drinks) menu with a good selection of beer, while you wait for your entree to come out. Tarahumaras has a nice lunch selection and they aren't afraid to be generous with avocado slices on your plate, which is always welcome, in my humble opinion. They offer up a nice low-carb menu instead of the standard giant serving of beans and rice, and you can get everything from ceviche to *guisado de carne,* a delicious beef stewed with onions, pepper, and garlic. For dessert skip the standard sopaipilla and order the churros, a freshly fried confection sprinkled with cinnamon and nestled between clouds of whipped cream and strawberry.

Two Olives Cafe, 201 N. Broadway St., Moore, OK 73160; (405) 895-6373; twoolivescafe.com; Sandwiches/Soups; $. A few words come to mind when you walk into Two Olives Cafe. "Charming" and "old-school" are some of them. Tricia Henderson opened this little darling of a place in Old Town Moore and it's a great place to visit in that area for lunch. The inside has been brought back to its beautifully historic, old-world interior and the menu is full of simple but tasty sandwiches and salads, including vegetarian options. Their soups are wonderful, especially the tomato basil soup! Their desserts get rave reviews, especially the cookies and the Rolo brownie. Everything seems very fresh at this little gem and if you lunch here, you will leave feeling just a little more relaxed and a little more at ease. Two Olives just leaves you with that cozy feeling.

Victoria's Pasta Shop, 327 White St., Norman, OK 73069; (405) 329-0377; Italian; $. With its hardwood floors and the typical campus corner hangout feel—after all, it's located a stone's throw away from the University of Oklahoma—this little Italian place might seem small but it has a large menu with delicious offerings at reasonable prices. But the pasta at Victoria's Pasta Shop has been

the culinary star for Norman and its surrounding area for years. Victoria's pasta is fresh with that coveted al dente bite to it, and while dishes might not be fancy, any meal you get here will be good.

And the portions are generous, my friends, very, very generous! Sit upstairs in the back behind the kitchen and breathe in wafts of Italian sauces and garlic bread while you wait. A local favorite choice is the Lasagna Roll. Fresh lasagna strips are wrapped around shrimp, spinach, and cheese and served with a harmony of marinara and Alfredo sauce. If you're going to a Sooner's football or basketball game or visiting the campus, try this place out.

Whispering Pines Inn, 7820 OK-9, Norman, OK 73026; (405) 447-0202; thewhisperingpinesinn.com; French/Fine Dining; $$$$. White tablecloths, stemware, antique chairs and bone china always make a diner feel special. How about sipping a sangria made with fresh grape juice from the restaurant's vineyard? Surround yourself in a beautifully gardened setting at the Whispering Pines Inn. Also a bed and breakfast, this little hidden gem is tucked away in a wooded area in Norman and surrounded by vineyards, gazebos, and darling cottages, and locals rave about it. The eatery offers up a really nice wine list and you'll need to break out your good duds (business casual) if you dine here as they have a suggested dress code. Chinda and Rany Kchao, both French continental chefs, have created a lovely thing in Whispering Pines. Be adventurous and try the ragout of escargots or be safe and try the salmon *en croûte*. Either way you go, it'll be superbly French and fantastic.

Cattlemen's Steakhouse, 1309 S. Agnew Ave., South Oklahoma City, Oklahoma City, OK 73108; (405) 236-0416; cattlemensrestaurant.com; Steak House; $$. Where else would be more appropriate for a good old-fashioned Oklahoma City steak house than smack dab in the middle of the city's stockyards? This legendary steak house has been open since 1910 and is the oldest running restaurant in Oklahoma! It first began as a feeding trough for hungry cowboys and stockyard workers and was one of the few places in later years that stayed open late enough to offer up some good drink offerings to the cowboys. Won in a gambling debt in 1945, ownership changed to Gene Wade and has since become the place most out-of-town guests have been advised they need to visit. Presidents, big-screen stars, and all sorts of greats have dined at Cattlemen's over the years, and you can too. Be brave and try the legendary lamb fries, or their steak soup, which also features that "special" masculine part of the steer, but the featured baby of the family at Cattlemen's is the steaks, hand cut in their own butcher shop then grilled up to your liking over a hot charcoal grill. Finish it off with a freshly baked pie slice, and you'll see why this place has stayed around for over a decade.

Dan's Old Time Diner, 8433 S. Western Ave., South Oklahoma City, Oklahoma City, OK 73139; (405) 634-8806; Burgers; $. Simple burgers. Simple hand-cut french fries straight off the potato. Add a little grilled onion to the mix and you've got something special. Then add in a topping and condiment bar and the fact that this place has been around since 1982 and has remained relatively the same. Well, then people really, really like what Dan's has been doing for the past three decades. Sit amidst a collection of Coca-Cola memorabilia, feast on these simple pleasures while drinking, what else, Coca-Cola, and this place won't break your budget. It is affordable at about $5 to $6 per person, making it a great place to stop and grab a burger and fries!

The Greek House, 768 Jenkins Ave., Norman, OK 73069; (405) 364-6300; Greek; $. Step into true Greek culture when you visit this gyro dive in Norman. Sit at the bar and watch the large spools of meat, glistening with slow-roasted juice, slowly wind around on the large metal rods that turn them to the heat. Watch one of the staff take a long flat knife and begin to strip off thin slices of the meat and toss it on a flat griddle to sizzle. Drooling yet? Then go visit The Greek House, where the ambience may not be fine dining, but the gyros are pure savory deliciousness. The restaurant was first opened for foreign students from the Middle East who longed for the taste of their back home eastern Mediterranean cuisine, and now everyone benefits. See why this Greek eatery has been around in Norman for over 30 years when you get a bite of one of those juicy gyros.

HOME-GROWN CHAINS: RON'S HAMBURGERS AND CHILI

Ron Baber opened his first Ron's Hamburgers and Chili (ronschili .com) in 1975 after quitting his day job and deciding to live his dream and open his own restaurant. Over 30 years later, there are 18 locations in Oklahoma City and Arkansas that serve up his wonderful hamburgers; many of the Ron's locations are franchises, but six spots are kept in the family and are owned by his children. His chili has been awarded four stars by the International Chili Society and the burgers were voted "Best Hamburger and Chili" by the *Urban Tulsa Weekly*. The philosophy at Ron's is to make a few things and make them really well. At Ron's you can get a variety of burgers, from single to double to jumbo. Try their sausage cheeseburger for a different twist, made with Owen's hot sausage and topped with hot pepper cheese. You can also get a fantastic country-fried steak at Ron's or a Frito chili pie topped with that famous chili. And to wash it down, get a big frosted mug of real draft root beer.

Legend's Restaurant, 1313 W. Lindsey St., Norman, OK 73069; (405) 329-8888; legendsrestaurant.com; Seafood/Steak House; $$$. This began as a pizza delivery service (Lemuel B. Legend's, Ltd.) at Norman's South Navy Base, and got you a pizza delivered by a little guy in an antique Rolls-Royce. Now, forty years later, it's evolved into a legendary steak house. Recognized by *Bon Appétit* magazine and *Southern Living* for their stellar desserts, Legends has been . . . well, a legend for more than 40 years in Norman. Owner Joe and Executive Chef Rebecca Sparks offer a menu that is a fresh and inviting lineup of pork, steak, seafood, fowl, and pasta dishes. They also serve a brunch Sunday from 10 a.m. to 3:30 p.m. featuring a Bloody Mary bar!

The Mont, 1300 Classen Blvd., Norman, OK 73071; (405) 329-3330; themont.com; Cafe; $. In 1976, three former Oklahoma University students and fraternity brothers reopened the building that was formerly The Monterrey restaurant. Nicknamed the Mont, this hangout has become legend around Norman, serving up some of the best exotic and mixed drinks around. Legendary is "The Swirl," a frozen margarita and sangria, swirled together. The Mont also offers up a full menu of burgers, sandwiches, and entrees along with daily house specials. After being open for almost 40 years, The Mont doesn't appear to be going away anytime soon!

Specialty Stores, Markets & Producers

Blue Bean Coffee, 13316 S. Western Ave., South Oklahoma City, Oklahoma City, OK 73170; (405) 735-5115. "Do the blue bean thing" is a bold statement on the menu behind the counter at Blue Bean Coffee. Sporting free Wi-Fi, notebooks on the table for you to doodle on, and also checkerboards painted right on the table, this is one of those places where you just want to get a good latte and settle in for some good company. French press, lattes, smoothies, mocha, scones, and other delicious baked goods, yes, they've got it all here. Blue Bean is the perfect coffee shop.

Crimson N Whipped Cream, 331 White St., Norman, OK 73069; (405) 307-8990; crimsonbakery.com. A large dining area, bright, high booths, along with brick-walled counters and hanging lights make this a favorite hangout for college students and bakery/coffeehouse customers in Norman. The cupcakes alone are a sight and taste to behold, but many are huge fans of the coffee as well, supplied by local roaster Elemental Coffee. The whoopie pies and baked goods change daily so visit the website if you have a preference, but no matter what day you go, you're sure to love this sweet treat eatery.

Custard Factory, 1000 E. Alameda St., Norman, OK 73071; (405) 360-6177. If you're a local Norman dweller or an out-of-town person, stop by the Custard Factory for a frozen and creamy delight. From concretes, like a tribute to nearby Oklahoma University aptly named Crimson and Cream (vanilla custard with strawberries and bananas), to seasonal flavors like pumpkin, the sweet offerings attract families who love to hang out here. The portions are generous and you can have something as crazy as a Rice Crispy concrete with marshmallow fluff and Rice Krispies cereal or just go classic and try a flavor on its own. But either way, stop in to the Custard Factory for a sweet and creamy concoction of goodness.

Dara Marie's Gift Boutique and Bakery, 1420 N. Porter Ave., Norman, OK 73071; (405) 364-3272. Friendly, smiling faces and tearoom-type food make this little gem in Norman a great place to visit. From fabulous baked goods to sandwiches to salads and spiced tea, you'll love a visit to Dara Marie's for lunch (or breakfast too for that matter!). The Reese's Peanut Butter Cookies are out of this world and if you visit this shop at just the right time, you can get them fresh out of the oven. Browse through the gift shop of candles, jewelry, clothing, and other gifts while picking up a delicious bite to eat!

Gray Owl Coffee, 223 E. Gray St., Norman, OK 73069; (405) 701-2929. Real cups, an eclectic atmosphere featuring mismatched thrift-style furniture, local artwork, magazines, books, and board games make this coffeehouse a favorite among locals. Oh, and there's coffee and tea as well. This is a wildly popular hangout for laptop-wielding Oklahoma University students hunkering down to study, and many coffee addicts head outside to the back patio to relax during nice weather. And for a special plus? Ask about the private lending library in the back, because Gray Owl is neighborly like that.

Downtown Oklahoma City

*Automobile Alley, Bricktown, Midtown, Deep Deuce &
Downtown Business District*

The neighborhood from NE 13th Street to NE 4th Street and just
west of Broadway and east to I-235 is the historic Automobile Alley
district and is the former marketplace of the automotive industry
in Oklahoma City. New businesses, residences, galleries, and of
course, eateries are starting to see the benefit of moving into this
area. With the Automobile Alley Main Street program, which aims to
develop the area as a "front door to downtown," new and exciting
dining opportunities are sure to come.

Bricktown is sometimes called the Entertainment District and
is just east of downtown. In the 1990s, Oklahoma City approved
the first of its MAPS projects to renovate downtown in this former
warehouse and railroad district. First up was construction of the

THE UNDERGROUND

Underneath downtown Oklahoma City lies a secret even many longtime Oklahoma City dwellers don't know about. Built in the early 1930s, this underground passageway was first named for Jack Conn, who renovated it in the 1970s, redesigned it, and called it The Conncourse. There is an almost mile-long tunnel system that links 16 blocks and over 30 buildings together. It is carpeted, painted in bright colors, has a lighting plan that has just been renovated, and has been renamed The Underground. The Invited Artists Gallery is now housed in there and displays featured Oklahoma artists. The Underground is open business days only from 6 a.m. to 8 p.m. For access points, you can check out the map at downtownokc.com.

Bricktown Ballpark and mile-long Bricktown Canal, which is now lined with numerous eateries, shops, and nightlife spots. Water taxis and horse-drawn carriages are often seen transporting folks around this happening area. Bricktown is bordered by the Oklahoma River to the south and I-235 to the east.

The Deep Deuce District is being restored to its glory days as a jazz hub by building a thriving new urban apartment complex, which now hosts several restaurants with entertainment and an art gallery.

The true downtown area of Oklahoma City features old buildings like the courthouse but also new things to see like the Devon Energy building; you can't miss it on the Oklahoma City downtown skyline as no building comes close to its height. With various hotels and prime office space, there are sure to be fabulous lunch and dinner spots always waiting for diners.

Becoming characteristic of all of downtown Oklahoma City, Midtown is also under a revitalization effort. Hip urban housing, sidewalk cafes, and outdoor events and festivals are included in this up-and-coming section of the city that extends from NW 13th Street south to 4th Street to Robinson Avenue and Classen Boulevard. The goal for this area is to have an energized, ethnically diverse area with great restaurants, shops, and art galleries. The eateries currently cropping up in this part of the city definitely fit the bill for this vision.

Foodie Faves

The Bar of Ludivine, 805 N. Hudson, Midtown District, Oklahoma City, OK 73102; (405) 778-6800; ludivineokc.com/bar; Cocktail Bar; $$. One of Oklahoma City's most beloved new restaurants also serves up some amazing cocktails. Slip through the door of the restaurant into the adjoining space and you'll feel truly special sipping on one of their organic cocktails. You really should stop in at the beginning of the work week and check out Ricky's $10 Blue Plate Mondays, because you can't go wrong with Ludivine's cuisine offerings. With your cocktail you'll get something wonderful like chicken and dumplings, and much of the food is locally grown and raised. But the highlight at the bar is truly the cocktail fare whipped up by their mixologist, and it most likely won't be anything like you've had before. Try the Hornet's Nest, mixed with saffron gin, honey, orange, baked apple bitters, and ginger beer. They also offer some great and very unusual beers like Young's Double Chocolate Stout and Pinkus Organic Hefeweizen. And of course, there is wine by the glass and bottle. Twice a month you can check them out and learn how to make some favorite cocktails at their Drinking School. Check their website for details.

Bolero Spanish Grill & Tapas Bar, 200 S. Oklahoma Ave., Ste. 140, Bricktown District, Oklahoma City, OK 73104; (405) 602-0652; bolerotapasbar.com; Spanish/Tapas; $$. Overlooking the river in downtown Bricktown, Bolero is a fun-filled tapas bar. Executive Chef Curtis Bramlett trained in New York City and worked in Miami for a period, where he developed a love for Spanish and Latin American food. He brings that love to his cuisine at Bolero by offering a menu of tapas or small dishes to be served typically with wine (Spanish wine, of course!). Try the delicious golden fried goat cheese drizzled with Tupelo honey or the artichoke frito with lemon-garlic aioli. If you're fortunate enough to dine during nice weather, Bolero turns their dining room into a covered patio of sorts by opening up the wall and letting in the fresh air. Bolero is located very close to the Harkins Bricktown Theater and directly in walking range of the canal. A perfect place to go with your honey or a group for a night on the town.

Bricktown Brewery, 1 N. Oklahoma Ave., Bricktown District, Oklahoma City, OK 73104; (405) 232-2739; bricktownbrewery.com; Brewpub; $$. You'd never know that this cool eatery once housed a candy factory. The building was opened in the early 1900s to churn out candy for quite some time. The Brewery came about in the eighties in its original form but recently underwent a major renovation on both the interior of the restaurant and on the menu, which boasts a great variety of Southwestern fare that more than likely is going to contain bacon. Try their Chopped and Chipped Nachos, loaded up with pulled pork tossed in bourbon sauce, bacon, beer BBQ sauce, and cheddar cheese. The nachos go splendidly with the Remington Red, a nicely balanced ale made at the brewery from a smooth toasted malt with a light fruitiness. With their one-of-a-kind Beer Tap Table, you can sit with your friends, watch a game, and have your very own choice of brew right in the middle of your table complete with four taps. They are also located inside Remington Park Racetrack on the casino floor at 1 Remington Place, Oklahoma City, OK 73111; (405) 419-4449.

Bricktown Burgers, 300 E. Main St., Bricktown District, Oklahoma City, OK 73104; (405) 232-4373; Burgers; $. Don't you just love a place that makes homemade burgers? Don't you just love an unpretentious setting with friendly down-to-earth people who offer you that burger? Bricktown Burgers sits in the midst of a trendy area in the heart of Bricktown and offers up just that. A nice thick and juicy burger cooked just a few different ways like onion-cooked, no onions, and with bacon, cheese, or a much-loved favorite around here, the Theta, which is a hamburger served with a hickory sauce with pickles and cheese. They also offer up a small sandwich menu along with hot dogs, french fries, and no fuss or frills. The worst part of going to Bricktown Burgers is that it is usually packed and finding a seat might be difficult!

Burger Rush, 119 N Robinson Ave., Lower Level Bay 6, Downtown District, Oklahoma City, OK 73102; (405) 605-7874; burgerrush.net; Burgers; $. This little burger place located in the food court of the Robinson Renaissance building is open only for lunch, but might just change the way you look at a burger. Don't let the word "burger" throw you off if you desire a sandwich other than ground beef, because Burger Rush has some wonderful sandwiches that masquerade under the name "burger." Andrew Hwang and Kevin Lee, whose culinary specialties are more Asian, offer up some truly unique sandwiches at Burger Rush. Maybe not truly considered a burger, their most popular item that folks rave about is the soft-shell crab burger, fried and layered soft-shell crab with slices of avocado and spicy mayo. They also have delicious regular and sweet potato fries and serve some naughty desserts like fried Twinkies and Snickers.

Cafe Do Brazil, 440 NW 11th St., Ste. 100; Midtown District, Oklahoma City, OK 73103; (405) 525-9779; cafedobrazilokc.com; Brazilian; $$. Located in the midtown section of town, the capacious white Spanish building is conspicuously unlike the rest of Oklahoma City's architecture. That's because it houses something different, including the cuisine inside. From their lunch specials to their weekend brunch, Cafe Do Brazil is a much buzzed-about place in Oklahoma City. Check out the board at the front of the restaurant for their daily specials or browse the menu for favorites like empanadas, ceviche or *feijoada,* (the Brazilian national dish) with its stew of black beans, sausage, and pork meat, served with collard greens, rice and *farofa (toasted manioc flour)*. Of special note is the little rooftop gem of a bar—Bossa Nova, where you can go after dinner and relax with friends. On particularly gorgeous nights, step outside to the open-roof patio bar and listen to live music.

Earl's Rib Palace, 216 Johnny Bench Dr., Bricktown District, Oklahoma City, OK 73104; (405) 272-9898; earlsribpalace.com; Barbecue; $$. Earl's Rib Palace has a slogan: "If you can find better BBQ, eat it!" We Oklahomans love us some Earl's! With seven locations around Oklahoma City, drop in for some smoked and tender brisket, pulled pork, ribs, bologna, chicken, polish sausage, hot links, or turkey. Before you go through the line and order, grab a cup and get your drink. Opt for the regular portions, which are quite filling in their own right, or the "light" sizes. They have some delicious sides as well, like crispy fried okra and coleslaw. My husband's favorite things to order at Earl's, however, are the cheddar burgers and the blackberry cobbler. The hearty, smoky burgers are delicious, and the blackberry cobbler? Served in a large bowl, topped with ice cream, and sprinkled with cinnamon sugar, it's worth the trip just for dessert!

1492: New World Latin Cuisine, 1207 N. Walker Ave., Midtown District, Oklahoma City, OK 73103; (405) 236-1492; 1492okc.com; Latin Fusion/Tex-Mex; $$. With menu items featuring ceviche, plantains, and yucca, you could venture off into the Tex-Mex menu, but why would you? 1492, opened by the Chavez brothers in 2007, does Latin fusion the right way, complete with a casually classy dining area, open, airy windows, fun Latin music, and a lengthy wraparound bar. The Latin menu is the way to go, and I highly recommend the Cuban *puerco criolla,* a Cuban pork shoulder stuffed with goodness like guava shells, prunes, and bacon (only served Thurs through Sat). And if you're used to bland, pale yellow *queso* typically served at Tex-Mex places, I encourage you to try the 1492 *queso* with beans, kicked-up beef, pico, and guacamole served with extra-thick tortilla chips for scooping it all up. After hours is fun at 1492, as the bar serves up a fabulous mint mojito.

Iguana Mexican Grill, 9 NE 9th St., Automobile Alley District, Oklahoma City, OK 73102; (405) 606-7172; iguanamexicangrill .com; Southwestern/Mexican; $$. Doesn't coral snake salsa sound intriguing? How about pork belly tacos? You can find both in this unique Mexican joint located in Automobile Alley. Chef Lee Bennett and owner Robert Painter, beloved by locals in Oklahoma City, have a little gem in Iguana Mexican Grill. From Tuesday $1 taco night, which boasts three regular flavors and weekly new offerings like roasted vegetable or quail with peach chutney, to the fried chicken and Champagne Mondays, Iguana always has something happening. But don't just go on Mondays or Tuesdays, because the full menu any other day is just as adventurous! From Chef Bennett's creations to fine wines and spirits connoisseur Rebecca Daley, whose mission it is to seek out and find the best tequila to be had, things at Iguana are always going to be delicious fun. You should try to attend one of Iguana's tequila dinners (but book fast, because the seats are gone in a flash). Iguana opened a second eatery called Iguana Café in Nichols Hills at 6482 Avondale Dr., Nichols Hills, OK 73116, (405) 463-2257.

James E. McNellie's Public House, 1100 Classmen Dr., Midtown District, Oklahoma City, OK 73103; (405) 600-1178; mcnelliesokc .com; Pub Food; $$. The comfort of a local pub straight out of Dublin is right here in Midtown, Oklahoma City. Feel right at home in this neighborhood gathering place while enjoying a selection of over 350 bottled beers and many options of single malt scotches. If

Guinness is your thing, you're going to have a hard time picking as they not only offer the traditional Guinness, but also several mixes as well. I especially love how they've moved our local Oklahoma breweries to the forefront of the menu and have an entire Oklahoma brew section devoted to Mustang, Marshall, Redbud, COOP, and Choc. Visit them on Firkin Fridays starting at 6 p.m. when they have a special pour that lasts until it runs out. Feast on some great pub grub as well, with everything from potato leek soup to fried pickles to spicy marinara sautéed black mussels and pub fries. You're going to just be a part of the gang at McNellie's.

Kaiser's American Bistro, 1039 N. Walker Ave., Midtown District, Oklahoma City, OK 73102; (405) 232-7632; kaisersbistro .com; Sandwiches/Ice Cream; $. Shaun Fiaccone recently reopened this more than 100-year-old ice cream shop. It's open for lunch and dinner, and you can have a wonderful bowl of soup, a Kaiser Big Bison Burger, or even Beer Battered Fish-and-Chips. You could also sit at the counter on an old-fashioned soda fountain stool and order a soda from the—what else?—an old-fashioned soda fountain. Families or sweethearts will love to go for a dessert date and taste Kaiser's hand-dipped ice cream, or milk shake treat from the ice-cream parlor. You can even get a grown-up version of an ice cream milk shake with their Spiked Milkshake or Soda Cocktail. They also have some vegetarian offerings like the roasted vegetable sandwich for those wanting something a bit healthier. I also can't neglect to tell you about their wonderful soups like the Grateful Bean Soup, a nod to a former name of the restaurant. Check out the Kaiser memorabilia while you're there and step back in time, if only for a moment.

Kamp's 1910 Cafe, 10 NE 10th St., Automobile Alley District, Oklahoma City, OK 73104; (405)-230-1910; kamps1910cafe.net; Breakfast/Sandwiches; $. Opened by the third generation Kamp of Kamp's grocery fame, Randy Kamp runs a cafe by day and wine and tapas bar by night housed in a quaint, historic building that sits near a set of railroad tracks that some of the menu items are aptly named for. One such item is the Wrong Side of the Tracks Reuben, one of their most popular sandwiches—perhaps because it's piled high with pastrami instead of corned beef. A must-try at Kamp's 1910 is the baked goods, especially the giant cupcakes. Breakfast offerings are hearty and full of down home goodness and also include a fresh fruit salad tossed with yogurt and herbs or oatmeal. In the evening, Kamp's converts to The Vineyard, a wine and tapas bar that's a nice place to wind down the evening.

Ludivine, 805 N. Hudson Ave., Automobile Alley District, Oklahoma City, OK 73102; (405) 778-6800; ludivineokc.com, facebook.com/ludivineokc; Farm to Table; $$$. Stop in at Ludivine and find out why chefs like Emeril Lagasse, Anthony Bourdain, and

CHEF SPOTLIGHT:
JONATHON STRANGER & RUSS JOHNSON

Recently nominated for the People's Best New Chef award by *Food & Wine* magazine, Jonathon Stranger and Russ Johnson, while still young in age, have already racked up numerous frequent-flyer points in the way of cuisine. Jonathon started out early cooking things with his grandfather, which grew into his true love of being a chef. Russ can't remember a time when he wasn't obsessed with food. Using their farm-to-table approach at **Ludivine** (p. 132), these two offer up some of the most magnificent masterpieces of local cuisine in Oklahoma.

Rick Bayless pick this place when passing through town. Ludivine's farm-to-table concept is as local as you can get. Utilizing as much produce, dairy, and meat (and recently foraged goodies!) as they can from around Oklahoma, Chefs Jonathon Stranger and Russ Johnson's menu varies according to what's available and what's in season. (See Chef Stranger's recipe for **Dock Soup** on p. 240.) Checking their Facebook page is always a good way to find out if the menu has been updated as well, and usually they have a video featuring their menu items that they update regularly. On Monday, check out their Rickey's Blue Plate Menu in their bar, where the special is always $10 and you can also enjoy a fresh drink prepared by their mixologist, like freshly made ginger beer. Also at the bar, enjoy a late night menu from 10 p.m. until 2 a.m. on Fri and Sat.

The restaurant is closed Sun and Mon but the bar is open Mon through Sat.

The Mantel Wine Bar & Bistro, 201 E. Sheridan Ave., Bricktown District, Oklahoma City, OK 73104; (405) 236-8040; themantelokc .com; Wine Bar, $$$$. Dark, classy high-cushioned booths, white tablecloths, low hanging lights, and an international wine list (36 by the glass and over 100 bottled) make this fine dining institution a wonderful place to dine alone or with friends. Listen to soft jazz as you browse the menu created by Executive Chef Gerald Harden and try to decide between one of their prime beef cuts, fresh seafood, or pasta options. Their spinach salad with raspberry, caramelized onions, and blue cheese is heavenly. I love that you can order roasted garlic from the appetizer menu drizzled with aged balsamic and olive oil. Try the pork tenderloin with asparagus and garlic potatoes sitting in the most fabulous Madeira wild mushroom cream sauce. Have a specific diet like gluten-free? Ask about their Special Request menu by calling ahead and explaining your dietary needs. Be warned, however, about dessert: You may want to split it as they are usually generously portioned, but we're not complaining.

Mickey Mantle's Steakhouse, 7 S. Mickey Mantle Dr., Bricktown District, Oklahoma City, OK 73104; (405) 272-0777; mickey mantlesteakhouse.com; Steak House/Seafood; $$$$. When out-of-towners come to Oklahoma City, they often go to Mickey Mantle's

CHEF SPOTLIGHT: DANIEL NEMEC

Daniel Nemec is the corporate executive chef for Kirby's Prime Steakhouse, **Mickey Mantle's Steakhouse** (p. 134), and Woodfire by Kirby's. Graduating from the Texas Culinary Academy in 1999 and being classically trained in French cuisine, he has cooked for such celebrities as Lady Bird Johnson, Lynn Cheney, Arnold Palmer, and John Travolta. He has worked at such prestigious restaurants as The Belgin and Girasole, both in Austin, Texas. Mickey Mantle's has become the restaurant most loved by visitors on business in the downtown area due to his creative and fantastic recipes. Chef Nemec also oversees five kitchens for Kirby's Prime Steakhouse and Woodfire, both located in Dallas, Texas. He has been the guest chef at the James Beard House as well. We are blessed to have this amazing chef right here in Oklahoma.

Steakhouse. From the baseball memorabilia to their actual street address (7, for Mickey Mantle's jersey number), there's a lot to love about Mickey Mantle's, including the cuisine. Prime aged steaks and exquisite seafood are just two of the reasons why happy customers return again and again. The wine list of over 400 wines is another. Executive Chef Daniel Nemec makes some fantastic cuisine and you'll want to try each and every item on the delicious menu. (See Chef Nemec's recipe for **Grilled Scallops with Watercress Salsa** on p. 248.)

Their towering Maryland-style crab cakes surrounded by a sea of beurre blanc are superb and their prime "cowboy cut" rib eye is to die for. Visit their 7 Lounge (where the OKC Thunder players often hang out) for a beautiful setting, an endless bar that seats scads of people, or sit in one of the silver-curtained privacy booths in the back. Live music is offered in the 7 Lounge on the weekend as well.

Museum Cafe, 415 Couch Dr., Downtown District, Oklahoma City, OK 73102; (405) 235-6262; okcmoa.com/eat; French; $$$. Within just a short stroll from the Civic Center, Stage Center, and Chesapeake Arena, and located on the ground floor of the Oklahoma City Museum of Art, is a lovely little dining place called the Museum Cafe. For lunch, they offer a delicious duck confit salad of baby spinach or try the open-faced crab cake sandwich. For dinner try the salmon carpaccio of paper-thin salmon lox, onions, pepper, and capers or the macaroni and cheese filled with shrimp, crab, langoustines, and sorrel pesto. No need to worry about wine as they have a huge assortment by the flight, glass, half bottle, or bottle, including many critically acclaimed imported and domestic wines. Sunday Brunch is filled with special cocktails and things like ratatouille, spinach- and chèvre-filled crepes. For dessert you must try the lemon crumb cake with its lemon curd and berry sauce. You can get afternoon tea from 3 p.m. to 5 p.m. Tues through Fri at the Cafe's beautiful bar made of black granite.

Nonna's Euro-American Ristorante & Bar, 1 Mickey Mantle Dr., Bricktown District, Oklahoma City, OK 73104; (405) 235-4410; nonnas.com; French/European; $$$. What started out as a truly scrumptious bakery has evolved into a classy and wonderful restaurant. And they own their own farm to grow their produce as well. Allow me to make a recommendation: Start your meal off with the Artichoke Duo. Composed of creamy artichoke dip surrounded by a pile of deep-fried artichoke hearts with a tart and creamy lemon dill aioli and crisp ciabatta wedges, it's the perfect way to begin your Nonna's experience. The Cedar Spring Bruschetta is served and prepared tableside with garden-ripe tomatoes, fresh basil, mozzarella, garlic, and rosemary olive oil. Nonna's relishes using fresh ingredients like Cedar Farms' tomatoes and pure cream in their tomato bisque and they incorporate the entire tomato, peel and all, to make it fresh and delicious. Don't leave before satisfying that sweet tooth—trying dessert is a must at Nonna's due to their bakery roots.

Pachinko Parlor, 1 NW 9th St., Automobile Alley District, Oklahoma City, OK 73102; (405) 601-8900; sushiokc.com, Japanese/ Sushi; $$$. Approach the patio on 9th Street and leave all your expectations of normal sushi at the door. When you visit Pachinko Parlor, you're going to see some menu items a little bit off the norm where sushi is concerned. With rolls like chicken curry and Philly cheese steak, non-sushi lovers will quickly become converts at this funky little place in Automobile Alley. There are also traditional sushi offerings so don't let that deter you! If you're in the mood for some Japanese food, they also offer noodle dishes like pad thai and Asian spaghetti, a mix of udon noodles, mushrooms, and a ginger chive pesto. The bar has a decidedly Asian twist as well, with sips like the Japanese Cherry Coke and the Great Panda Margarita. For lunch they have some fantastic sandwiches and for dinner, a great entree menu offering things like five-spice pork tenderloin with soy butter. Take a date and get their Service for Two, a chef's tasting menu with wine pairing.

Purple Bar, 1 Mickey Mantle Dr., Bricktown District, Oklahoma City, OK 73104; (405) 235-4410; purplebarokc.com; Pub Food; $$. The Purple Bar is a mirage of psychedelic colors and lights in a classy atmosphere and is on the second level of **Nonna's Euro-American Ristorante & Bar** in Bricktown (p. 137). They have an upscale appetizer in the Mango Crab Stack with its layers of avocado, mango salsa, and crab remoulade, served with basil aioli drizzled over all and complete with ciabatta crisps to scoop it up. Want something a little more manly? Try the Kobe sliders topped with bacon, house-cured and smoked right at Nonna's and nestled alongside some *pommes frites*. There is also a lovely artisan cheese selection from which you can pick and choose while sipping on your choice of wine. The Purple Bar also has a wonderful selection of cocktails like their Spicy Antipasti, a kicked up Bloody Mary with a skewer of antipasti. You can't visit the Purple Bar without trying their signature Purple Bar Tini, a martini made with three liquors, grenadine, lime juice, and club soda. Gaze out over the twinkling lights of Bricktown as you socialize with your best friends at the Purple Bar.

Stella, 1201 N. Walker Ave., Midtown District, Oklahoma City, OK 73103; (405) 235-2200; stellaokc.com; Italian/Pizza; $$$. Winner of Best New Restaurant in the *Oklahoman*'s Readers' Choice Awards in 2011, Lori Tyler has brought upscale Italian food to midtown Oklahoma City. Her food centers on the wood-burning brick oven and it turns outs delectable offerings like thin, crispy, oblong Roman-style pizzas, and also the meats to top their pastas and salads. Fine-dining settings mix with vintage old-world walls and make you feel special while you dine on a starter of grilled asparagus topped with a fried quail egg and a tart vinaigrette with truffle oil. Main dishes range from veal osso buco to grilled swordfish, and their bread comes from nearby Prairie Thunder Bakery. Stella also offers a lengthy wine selection and signature old-school cocktails. Try them on Sunday for brunch or sit at the bar during their happy hour and enjoy half-price starters and wine. You'll feel old-world Italian at Stella and you'll enjoy it.

Tapwerks Ale House & Cafe, 121 E. Sheridan Ave., Bricktown District; Oklahoma City, OK 73104; (405) 319-9599; Pub Food; $$. If beer is your thing, you're going to love Tapwerks. Choose from over 200 beers on tap or 100 bottles in a setting styled after an old English pub. Downstairs is a smoke-free restaurant while upstairs is the smoking lounge and bar complete with library, pool tables, dart boards, and jukebox. The specialty is their herbed, oven-roasted chicken, but be warned, there is limited availability as it goes quickly! Of course there are also offerings like Fuller's London Pride Battered Fish-and-Chips and an Oktoberfest-style bratwurst with mustard cream sauce. Here you might have a problem choosing what to pair it with as they have virtually every brew you can possibly think of from bocks and doppelbocks to porters and pale lagers and they're from all over the world. Can't decide on one? Try one of their sampler trays like the German Tray or the Hefe-Weizen Tray to acquaint you with some new brews you may not have tried. Head over to Tapwerks on Friday and Saturday to listen to live music.

Whiskey Chicks, 115 E. Reno Ave., Bricktown District, Oklahoma City, OK 73104; (405) 228-0087; whiskeychicksokc.com; Pub Food; $$. Vintage is all the rage right now so it would stand to reason that a vintage cocktail place would be pretty doggone cool. Want an old-fashioned cocktail like a Sazerac, a sidecar or a mint julep? And what could be better than some down-home pub food? If fried is your thing you can choose between fried pickles, okra, or jalapeños. There are also grilled chicken wings with four of Whiskey Chicks' signature sauces like Whiskey Glaze or Honey Buffalo. Head on over to Whiskey Chicks where there's always a special in the drink department and while you're at it, listen to live entertainment, or play trivia and have a great time.

Landmarks

Johnny's Lunchbox, 413 W. Sheridan Ave., Downtown District, Oklahoma City, OK 73102; (405) 232-9409; johnnyslunchbox.com; Sandwiches/Burgers; $. For over fifty years, Johnny's Lunchbox has been serving up some simply fabulous food in downtown Oklahoma City. On any given day you might see men in suits or faded jeans crowding in to get a great made-from-scratch home-cooked dish or a Reuben sandwich with homemade Thousand Island dressing. This place is home cooking at its best and it's no wonder why it's been around so long. You can also get a piece of down-home goodness by trying their custard pie. It's a Southern favorite and it tastes just like something grandma would make.

Specialty Stores, Markets & Producers

The Beatnix Cafe, 136 NW 13th St., Midtown District, Oklahoma City, OK 73103; (405) 604-0211; thebeatnixcafe.com. Their Facebook page brags "we are pretty boss baristas," and once you try a cup of their joe, you'll have to admit it's true. Need a great cup of coffee, with perhaps a Beatnix Bongo Bar, an all-natural house-made energy bar with oatmeal, pecans, almonds, flaxseed meal, honey, molasses, and peanut butter? Head on over to The Beatnix Cafe.

Enjoy free Wi-Fi while sampling their homemade soups and deli sandwiches. Try the Roast Beef Knuckle Sandwich, which is piled high with roast beef and cheddar cheese or the tomato basil bisque. The ever-popular favorite among locals is the Made in the Shade Chicken Salad Sandwich, featuring pulled chicken, grapes, walnuts, celery, green onions, and a not-too-heavy dressing. Specials change daily, so check out their chalkboard and order up.

Brown's Bakery, 1100 N. Walker Ave., Midtown District, Oklahoma City, OK 73103; (405) 232-0363. Around for over 60 years, Brown's Bakery offers up a plethora of doughnuts, cookies, pastries, breads, and pies. Try their legendary sausage rolls or apple fritters. You can order anything from a king's cake for Mardi Gras to pumpernickel bread, and don't leave without trying their sour cream doughnuts!

Coffee Slingers, 1015 N. Broadway Ave., Automobile Alley District, Oklahoma City, OK 73102; (405) 606-2763; coffeeslingers.com. Coffee Slingers sits in a simple red-brick building in Automobile Alley. Their emphasis on contemporary and organic offerings lends a young and fresh atmosphere, which is perfect for what Coffee Slingers does best: coffee. Cups are individually French pressed per order and they offer VillaCipres from South America, Malacara from El Salvador, and El Socorro from Guatemala. Fresh baked goods to enjoy with your steaming cup of java are also on offer.

Earth to Urban Local Food Hub, 1235 SW 2nd St., Downtown District; Oklahoma City, OK 73108. Venture a little bit southwest of Bricktown and you'll find Earth to Urban Local Food Hub, open only Wed through Sun from 1 p.m. to 6 p.m. Located in the old-school farmers' market, Earth to Urban is the beloved brain-

child of Matthew Burch of Urban Agrarian and April Herrington of Earth Elements. What this means for Oklahomans or visitors is that you can now get the benefits of scads of locally grown and produced products, produce, and meats and dairy all under one roof. You'll always find whatever is in season in produce, and you'll also find some wonderful products from breads to salsas to preserves. Earth to Urban is an excellent meeting of the minds and we customers get to reap all of the benefits.

1st Edition Cafe & Espresso Bar, 300 Park Ave., Downtown District, Oklahoma City, OK 73102; (405) 605-8347. Some of the best coffee, espresso, lattes, and macchiatos in town can be found at 1st Edition. Located inside the downtown library, 1st Edition also offers up a fun-filled menu with delights like mulligatawny soup; paninis named after famous poets like the Whitman, featuring marinated steak, tomato, swiss cheese, and basil pesto; and pizzas like the Hobbit, which is a classic Margherita pizza served on herbed flatbread.

Midtown Farmers' Market, 1000 N. Lee Ave., Midtown District, Oklahoma City, OK 73102 (East parking lot of St. Anthony's Hospital). This market is a unique farmers' market operated by Urban Agrarian's Matthew Burch (there's that name again!). There is one centralized checkout for the local produce and meats, like grass-fed Kobe beef. There are also numerous other offerings like cheeses, gourmet garlic, herbs, local eggs, and even orchids. Look for the big white tent in the parking lot May through Oct on Friday from 2:30 to 7 p.m. From Oct through Apr they have an order kiosk on the east side of the building. Simply put, I love any of Matt's farmers' market locations, and the Midtown Market is no exception.

Pinkitzel Cupcakes and Candy, 150 N. EK Gaylord Blvd., Bricktown District, Oklahoma City, OK 73102; (405) 235-7465; pinkitzel.com. Like an old fashioned—but large at 5,000 square feet—charming candy store, Pinkitzel Cupcakes and Candy always leaves you with a smile and a satiated sweet tooth. The shop sports black-and-white checkerboard floors and long glass bins filled to the brim with every type of candy you could possibly imagine. Try one of their many flavors of cupcakes with their signature swirled icing. Fancy a beverage to wash all that sugar down? Pinkitzel's offers French press coffee, hot chocolate, and Stewart's cream sodas. Their name is a playful combination of pink and *kitzel* (which means "tickle" in Yiddish), so basically Pinkitzel means "tickled pink," and you're sure to feel that way when you visit. Pinkitzel has a second location at 1389 E. 15th St., Edmond, OK 73103; (405) 330-4500.

Prairie Thunder Bakery, 1114 Classen Dr., Midtown District, Oklahoma City, OK 73103; (405) 602-2922; prairiethunderbaking .com. Located in the Plaza Court Building, Prairie Thunder Bakery is John McBryde's dream after quitting his full-time job of several years as an oil and gas man. Thank goodness he had that dream, as Oklahoma City is all the better for it. Artisan breads on offer here are hand-formed just as you'd see in Europe using old world–style recipes and technique. The pastries are just as gorgeous to look at as they are to taste. It's no wonder that many of the local restaurants use Prairie Thunder's bread instead of making their own. They also have some fabulous sandwiches, soups, and salads for lunch at their cafe, so stop in, grab some lunch, and take some wonderful baked goods home with you for later.

Sara Sara Cupcakes, 7 NW 9th St., Automobile Alley District, Oklahoma City, OK 73102; (405) 600-9494; sarasarabakery.com. Sara Sara is a simple cupcake house located in the ever-popular 9th Street corridor. Folks like to grab some sushi at **Pachinko Parlor**

(p. 137), or a taco at **Iguana Mexican Grill** (p. 130), and then head over for dessert to Sara Sara. I love the Sara's Cinnamon Roll cupcake and the cappuccino cupcake but they also offer a savory rendition in the bacon, egg, and cheese cupcake. Coffee, tea, and espresso are on the menu but I love to grab a frosted mug out of the freezer and get an ice-cold glass of milk offered at their milk bar. You have your choice of plain, chocolate, strawberry, and the seasonal offering; if you time your visit just right, their creamsicle flavor is a must-try.

Learn to Cook

Table One, 611 N. Broadway, Automobile Alley District, Oklahoma City, OK 73102; (405) 607-8131; facebook.com/TableOneOkc. The concept of Table One, the product of Chef Ryan Parrott and Chef Jonathon Krell, is super cool. It's a private dinner party where the chefs do cooking demonstrations, and you the lucky diner get to feast on the prepared items. Located in a studio-type room in Automobile Alley, the brick walls and stained concrete flooring create a unique space with one large table by the high glass windows out front, where you can sit and dine after the demonstration. Chefs Parrott and Krell will also do an 8- to 10-course dinner for small groups. If you have a hankering for something special and want to get a group together for a demonstration, you can't go wrong with Table One.

Tulsa

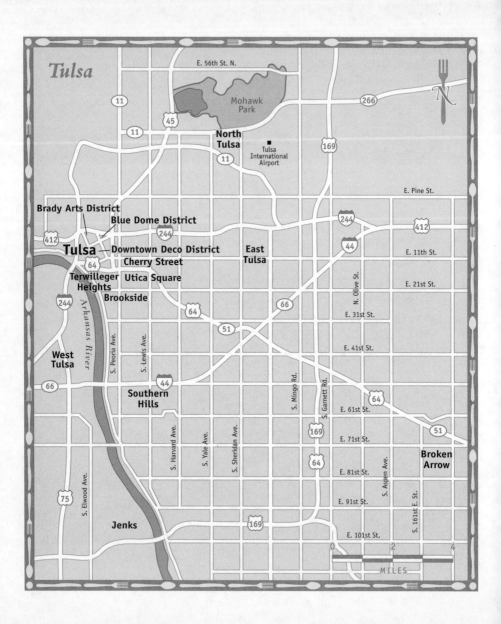

Tulsa

E. 56th St. N.

Mohawk Park

North Tulsa

Tulsa International Airport

E. Pine St.

Brady Arts District

Blue Dome District

Tulsa

Downtown Deco District

Cherry Street

Terwilleger Heights

Utica Square

Brookside

East Tulsa

E. 11th St.

E. 21st St.

N. Olive St.

E. 31st St.

E. 41st St.

S. Peoria Ave.

S. Lewis Ave.

West Tulsa

Southern Hills

S. Harvard Ave.

S. Yale Ave.

S. Sheridan Ave.

S. Mingo Rd.

S. Garnett Rd.

E. 61st St.

E. 71st St.

Broken Arrow

S. Aspen Ave.

S. 161st E. St.

E. 81st St.

E. 91st St.

S. Elwood Ave.

Jenks

E. 101st St.

0   2   4

MILES

Arkansas River

Tulsa

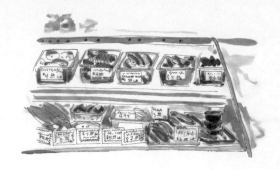

Tulsa began in the late 1800s as a cattle industry town when the railroad was built through it. The city began to draw crowds as large swaths of the American population began to move west. It later became a boomtown with the discovery of oil and it was during this period that Tulsa truly thrived and grew. A colossal plan to beautify the city began in the late 1950s and earned the city in the heart of Green Country the title of "Most Beautiful City." Tulsa later shook off its reputation as just a cow and oil town as aerospace, telecommunications, manufacturing, construction, high technology, health care, education, transportation, and energy businesses popped up all over the landscape.

Progress continued off and on during those years since and in 2003, city leaders began a drive for the passage of Vision 2025, and now an updated Downtown Tulsa Master Plan to revitalize the downtown Tulsa area in a variety of ways including connecting the city's waterways and updating the city's gateways and designs. There is a river project being planned as well much like Oklahoma City has, where eateries and retail would thrive once finished. Culture is rich in Tulsa and they are proud to boast about the Philbrook and Gilcrease Museums, the Tulsa Zoo, the Tulsa Ballet, Tulsa Opera, and the Tulsa Symphony Orchestra. Music and nightlife thrive here with many festivals and cultural events, and there's a vibrant food scene that boasts innovative, creative cuisine. I hope you'll take a ride along with me into the Tulsa districts and enjoy every tasty moment of it.

Tulsa

Blue Dome, Brady Arts, Brookside, Cherry Street, Downtown Deco, Utica Square, Terwilleger Heights & West District

The Blue Dome district is aptly named after an old blue-domed building that's been around since 1924 and located at the corner of 2nd Street and Elgin Avenue on the eastern side of downtown. It's the center of nightlife in downtown Tulsa and you will find numerous popular hangouts and eateries here, many of which feature local bands and nighttime music. It is also widely known for the Blue Dome Arts Festival in July and for the Diversafest Music Fest and Festival.

The red-bricked historic district of Brady Arts is one of the oldest in Tulsa, and owes its origin to its direct proximity to the railroad. Named for one of the pioneers of Tulsa, Wyatt Tate Brady, the Brady Arts district is the home of Cain's Ballroom, a unique concert venue that brings in all sorts of bands to Tulsa, and is an eclectic mix of old restored buildings as well as a new collection of restaurants, bars, and art galleries that have recently cropped up due to continued restoration going on in the area. This district is roughly bordered by East and West Cameron Streets and East and West Archer Streets from north to south, and North Denver Avenue and North Boulder Avenue from east to west.

The Brookside District is a very popular shopping and entertainment area in Midtown Tulsa. You'll find Brookside extending from the Arkansas River east to Lewis Avenue and then heading south to 51st Street and Interstate 44, but most of the food scene happens on South Peoria Street, specifically between 1st and 41st Streets.

Most of the entertainment quarter known as Cherry Street is actually located on 15th Street, between Peoria and Utica. This main strip of the Cherry Street district is noted for its dining. It is by far one of my favorite places to visit in Tulsa for the food scene and atmosphere. It also is the home to one of the best farmers' markets in Tulsa as well.

During the roaring twenties, the Downtown Deco district began to thrive due to its close proximity to the railroad. This district is located between 1st and 8th Streets and Cincinnati and Denver. There is a major plan for new development in this area and it will be one to watch for new eateries popping up in the future.

Tucked away in the heart of Midtown, the Terwilleger Heights district sports a cascade of elegant, vintage homes and buildings that date back to 1940 or earlier. While relatively small, this area of Tulsa houses some quaint, old-school eateries that have stood the test of time.

While not a formal district, Utica Square is a development between 21st Street and 22nd Place and between Yorktown Avenue and Utica Avenue. This lovely area is a hub of upscale shopping, bistros, and beautiful parks.

Foodie Faves

Andolini's Pizza, 1552 E. 15th St., Cherry Street District, Tulsa, OK 74120; (918) 728-6111; andopizza.com; Pizza/Pasta; $$. Andolini's is one of the hippest pizza places you'll ever visit. Brothers Mike and Jim Bausch have created a masterpiece in Tulsa, both inside the funky and artsy pizza house and with the pizzas they serve. There is no freezer or microwave here as everything is fresh or of the absolute best quality possible. These ingredients range from D.O.P. San Marzano tomatoes to pistachio pesto and speck, and it is exciting to witness this place using incredible food-lover's ingredients on their pizzas. Try the DeMarco of Brooklyn, with D.O.P. San Marzano tomatoes, fresh mozzarella, fresh basil, Pecorino Romano, and drizzled nicely with olive oil. The macaroni and cheese is to die for. Enjoy one of the four taps featuring local beer or a bevy of bottled beer choices as well. The kids can play with pizza dough while you wait and guests get to sign the back of the menus. There is a second location at 12140 E. 96th St. North, Owasso, OK 74055.

BBD Brookside By Day, 3313 S. Peoria Ave., Brookside District, Tulsa, OK 74105; (918) 745-9989; brooksidebyday.com; Breakfast; $. If you're from in or out of town, chances are you're going to need a good, hearty breakfast at some point, and Brookside By Day is the place to go for a no fuss, just-like-your-mama-made kind of breakfast. Hankering for a hearty omelet? Try the Lorraine which is heaped full of ham, bacon, onion, and topped with some melted swiss cheese. Want something a little different? Try their Basic Murrito, a breakfast burrito stuffed with scrambled eggs, sausage, green onions, and cheddar and served with fresh guacamole and home fries. This trendy Tulsa diner is usually packed full on the weekends so arrive early if you are looking for a home-cooked breakfast. They also serve up a mean flat-griddled hamburger and some outstanding fries and onion rings for lunch as well.

Biga Italian Restaurant, 4329 S. Peoria Ave., Brookside District, Tulsa, OK 74105; (918) 743-2442; bigaitalianrestaurant.com; Italian; $$. Owners Tuck and Kate Curren opened this charming little Italian trattoria over 10 years ago. Tuck is the chef but he's also an instructor at Rogers State University's culinary school. Chef Tuck's students bake the bread for the restaurant and it comes out crusty, hot, and fresh with a bowl of delicious olives. You can dine in the quaint and classy dining room with its soft candlelight and wine bottle–lined shelves, or opt to sit on one of two patios and dine alfresco. Start out your meal with a bowl of steamed mussels with tomato and basil and then move on to some fabulous pasta like the Spinach Handkerchiefs with roasted tomatoes and peppered mascarpone cheese. The eatery has a prix-fixe dinner, with an appetizer, main course, and dessert at a bargain $20. Whatever you decide to order, Biga has a nice offering of wines to sip along with it. Reservations are recommended ahead of time—this small space fills up fast.

Blue Moon Bakery & Cafe, 3512 S. Peoria Ave., Brookside District, Tulsa, OK 74105; (918) 749-7800; bluemoonbakerycafe .com; Sandwiches/Bakery; $. From the runners that stop into this quaint neighborhood cafe to parents of small children, everyone is comfortable dropping by and hanging out while eating some great food at Alan Fusco and Kim Nelson's place. From their collection of salt and pepper shakers, many of them donated by loyal patrons, to the art on the wall by local artists, these two have created a hangout for locals that is also a wonderful dining joint as well. Feast on their Reuben sandwich, where the corned beef is cured in house and served on homemade bread. Try their tamales on Saturday or something else from their ever-changing menu based on what's happening that week—you can't go wrong with any of Blue Moon's dishes.

Brady Tavern, 201 N. Main St., Brady Arts District, Tulsa, OK 74103; (918) 949-9801; bradytavern.com; Pub Food; $$$. Located in the old Fox Hotel building in the Brady Arts District, Chef Grant

Vespasian's restaurant creates a unique twist on tavern food in a setting that is reminiscent of an old English pub. Vespasian often uses the newly popular *sous vide* method of cooking, and he also gourmets his pub fare up a bit by offering some fantastic menu items such as Bacon Popcorn and a Deviled Egg Trifecta, with three offerings of deviled eggs like traditional, Southwestern and Asian, which involves a little wasabi. Try the *sous vide*–cooked tenderloin with a side of duck-fat fries. But the Tavern Burger is beloved by all and probably the most popular item on the menu. The patty is a combination of house-ground short ribs and brisket and it comes topped with Stilton cheese and a mushroom cream sauce that's to die for. For dessert, try one of pastry chef David Robuck's creations and have one of mixologist Tony Collin's special creations of old throwback cocktails.

The Brook Restaurant, 3401 S. Peoria Ave., Brookside District, Tulsa, OK 74105; (918) 748-9977; brookrestaurant.com; Pub Food; $. Ever want to dine inside an old movie theater? That's what you can do at The Brook Restaurant. The marquee outside displays specials instead of movie titles and might boast something to draw you in like daily drink specials or food fare loved by all tailgaters. Sports lovers will love this place, where you can get loaded cheese fries, The Brook's specialty, or families can grab some Southwest chicken nachos and then continue on with some of their notable burger choices. They even have a meatless burger for vegetarians made of black beans, rice, corn, and green chiles. The aforementioned loaded fries are covered in bacon, jalapeños, and chives and have become a Tulsa staple among locals. Check their webpage for daily drink specials and visit them on Thursday for half-price wine offerings. There is a second location at 7727 East 91st St., Tulsa, OK 74133; (918) 392- 9977.

Cafe Samana, 3807 S. Peoria Ave., Brookside District, Tulsa, OK 74105; (918) 742-3559; facebook.com/cafesamana; Vegetarian; $. Tracy Caton, owner of Cafe Samana, describes her restaurant as "upscale hippy" and it suits Cafe Samana's description to a T. The eclectic interior is a hodgepodge of mix-n-match tables and chairs, there is local art adorning the walls, and the food is organic and mostly vegetarian, although there are a few meat dishes that include chicken and fish. Daily offerings of wholesome, locally sourced ingredients can best be seen on their Facebook page, but there is also the set menu as well with offerings like fantastic, creamy and warm artichoke spread, served with fresh vegetables and sourdough bread baked by local Farrell bakery. There are vegan offerings as well, like the marinated Vegan Brat topped with organic sauerkraut and the Asparagus Bundles wrapped in marinated chard. Tracy's love for baking shines through in her daily offering of baked wonders like lemon ginger cupcakes.

Cosmo Cafe & Bar, 3334 S. Peoria Ave., Brookside District, Tulsa, OK 74105; (918) 933-4848; cosmo-cafe.com; Sandwiches/Soup/ Vegan; $. Cosmo is a truly fun hangout for young and happening

HOME-GROWN CHAINS: SONIC

Bigger and better than ever after 50 years, Sonic (sonicdrivein .com) is one of the major players in the drive-in business. In fact, it has become the largest drive-in chain in America. Started in 1953 in Shawnee, Oklahoma, by Troy Smith, Sonic's core value is "Surprise and Delight," and you will be delighted at any one of their 3,500 drive-ins. Drive up, push the red button, and order one of their specialties from an old classic like a foot-long coney dog, and fried pickle chips, to a new invention like Sweet Potato Tots. Burgers, fries, onion rings, and milk shakes along with old standbys like cherry limeade and slushies make this drive-in chain near and dear in all Oklahomans' hearts.

people in Brookside. A giant Scrabble wall spells out words like "Cosmopolitan" and "Lounge." Underneath it are shelves with scads of board games that you can take with you to a table and play with your friends. A funky lit bar snakes around the front of the eatery where locals love to hang out and get one of their signature drinks, like the Lush, a delicious blend of orange vodka, triple sec, strawberry schnapps, white cranberry juice, pineapple juice, and Sprite. Snack on one of their items off their bar snacks menu like nacho dishes or "bites," Cosmo's take on kicked-up bruschetta with things like shaved roast beef or avocado, herbed cream cheese, and fresh or marinated veggie toppings. They also have vegan and gluten-free menu items and some awesome hot or cold sandwiches, salads, and even fruit and cheese or meat and cheese platters.

Crow Creek Tavern, 3554 S. Peoria Ave., Brookside District, Tulsa, OK 74105; (918) 749-9100; crowcreektavern.com; Pub Food; $$. This pub-like biker bar is housed in a unique stone building and offers an enclosed patio complete with a fireplace. Their daily specials are good values, especially the Tuesday Crow Burger at $4. No biker bar would be complete without beer, and Crow Creek offers 15 on tap and many bottled imports as well. Check their website for their weekly schedule of live music and feast on something off the menu like homemade fried pickles or a 28-day aged Black Angus prime rib. For the lady biker who may want something lighter, there are offerings like the black bean burger and a wine menu to please.

Dalesandro's, 1742 S. Boston Ave., Terwilleger Heights District, Tulsa, OK 74199; (918) 582-1552; dalesandros.com; Italian; $$$. Twinkle lights line the window and contribute to the soft lighting and romantic atmosphere in this cozy Italian eatery. There is a large oval bar that is the focal point of the dining room and is a popular gathering spot for chat-
ting. Former professional soccer player Sonny Dalesandro will eventually make his rounds around the kitchen and dining area of the res- taurant his father started over 21 years ago. If you visit Dalesandro's you must try their Caesar

salad with roasted red peppers. It is proclaimed by Tulsa foodies as perhaps the best Caesar salad in the city. Twinkle lights are also outside on the quaint raised patio, and you can dine alfresco while feasting on one of their most beloved dishes, the swordfish piccata. This dish is the star of the menu and the fish is hand-cut, breaded in herbs, sautéed in butter, and nestled in piccata sauce. This buttery fish is incredible, light, and luscious.

Dilly Deli, 402 E. 2nd St., Blue Dome District, Tulsa, OK 74120; (918) 938-6382; dillydelitulsa.com; Cafe/Deli; $$. The artsy folk love Dilly Deli in Tulsa, and visit them once and you'll understand why. This eclectic little deli houses brightly colored walls and mismatched painted chairs and tables, and a bevy of organic and locally sourced culinary delights that come in the form of breakfast, lunch, and dinner dishes. For weekend brunch, try their Bloody Mary made with house-infused vodka. Dilly Deli serves up their sandwiches on locally made bread from Farrell's Family Bread bakery. Going for breakfast? Try the Jed, a cinnamon roll that the menu boasts is "as big as your head" and guess what? It is! And for lunch, try the Brown-Eyed Girl, a grilled chicken sandwich served with brie and lemon-basil mayo. Dine out on the patio where you can sit in an old car or play bocce ball with your honey. You'll see what makes this a hotspot for Tulsa foodies.

Doc's Wine and Food, 3509 S. Peoria Ave., Brookside District, Tulsa, OK 74105; (918) 949-3663; docswineandfood.com; Cajun/

Creole; $$$. Doc's Wine and Food (not to be confused with Doc's in Sapulapa) is a wonderful place to go for Cajun cuisine. From their flower-potted patio with yellow umbrella-topped tables to the cool atmosphere inside, this eatery has become a giant hit for diners in Brookside. Chef Ian Van Anglen has a creatively wonderful menu consisting of three types of oysters, fried, fresh, or topped with some delectable ingredients. Dishes include Cajun fried chicken and pan-seared duck breast with Creole seasoning and *maque choux*. The weekend brunch menu has a scrumptious offering of dishes like shrimp and grits—three pepper and goat-cheese grits, to be exact—and they have a wonderful wine menu with wines from Napa, Italy, New Zealand, and France among other sources. You can't leave Doc's without trying their bread pudding topped with bananas Foster.

The Doghouse, 1101 S. Detroit Ave., Downtown District, Tulsa, OK (918) 810-9330; doghousetulsa.com; Hot Dogs, $. Josh Lynch has a deep love for the hot dog, and it is evident when you visit The Doghouse in downtown Tulsa. The large chalkboard menus on the wall boast of 65 toppings and 10 different sausages to choose from. There are toppings ranging from jalapeño relish to raspberry jam. There are also a few vegetarian offerings like the falafel dog and the vegetarian dog, topped with grilled portobello mushrooms. Check out the live bands that play on a wooden stage in the corner of the parking lot from time to time, and sit at a picnic table and enjoy a dog outside. You can pick from a themed hot dog menu or create your own dog from the huge list of toppings. Try the Tulsa Dog with jalapeño relish, BBQ sauce, bacon, and cheese. The Doghouse also has a food truck and several stands open at Cain's Ballroom.

El Guapo's Cantina, 332 E. 1st St., Blue Dome District, Tulsa, OK 74120; (918) 382-7482; elguaposcantina.net; Tex-Mex; $$. Another of Elliot Nelson's (the McNellie group) endeavors, El Guapo's Cantina is a three-story eatery offering up some mighty good Tex-Mex fare. The decor changes depending on which floor you dine on but if it's nice weather, opt for the roof (El Guapo's is Tulsa's only rooftop restaurant). The Southwestern fare here offers diners some options ranging from authentic Mexican with the Alambres to their biggest seller—the Wet Burrito, which could easily feed two people. Being a fish taco lover, I recommend the grilled mahi mahi fish tacos served up with their scrumptious red chile aioli and jalapeño slaw. El Guapo's also does guacamole up just right and I'm a big fan of their *ceviche de camaron,* a luscious mix of shrimp, tomatoes, and avocado all served in a chilled and spicy tomato-based juice. Bars are offered on every floor to serve up tequila, *cervezas,* specialty drinks, and wine.

Elote Cafe, 514 S. Boston Ave., Downtown Deco District, Tulsa, OK 74103; (918) 582-1403; elotetulsa.com; Organic Mexican; $. Jeremy and Libby Auld have something truly unique in Elote Cafe and Catering by way of an organic Mexican restaurant. This couple, who are one-half business manager (Jeremy), one-half chef

(Libby), opened Elote Cafe in 2008 and Chef Libby, who returned to her roots after interning at Rick Bayless's Frontera Grill and Topolobampo in Chicago, specializes in whipping up some fabulous authentic and healthy Mexican dishes. The restaurant also boasts a very green and eco-friendly reputation as well. Their fresh ingredients, many of which are sourced locally, include meats organically grown and raised right here in Oklahoma. Start off your Elote experience with an appetizer of Fresh Fruit Pico Bites, crisp tortillas topped with a sweet jalapeño mousse and fresh fruit and then move on to one of the wonderful entrees like the salmon tacos covered in cilantro lime glaze. For dessert don't walk out without sampling a seasonal flan or a chocolate butternut squash empanada.

Fassler Hall, 304 S. Elgin Ave., Downtown District, Tulsa, OK 74120, (918) 576-7898; fasslerhall.com; German; $. It's Oktoberfest every day at Fassler Hall. Dine as you might over in Europe with communal seating, as the dining room is a massive, wide-open space with large, wooden picnic tables. Fassler Hall has over 25 offerings of German beer to enjoy while also feasting on their delicious authentic German dishes. Snack on a fresh, hot pretzel served with homemade spicy mustard while you wait for your meal to come out. And what could go better with all that beer than a brat? Fassler Hall offers several varieties of sausage from habañero chicken sausage to their well-loved lamb sausage. Everything is homemade here including the sauerkraut and the hand-cut duck fat–fried french fries. Check their website for local live-music nights and entertainment. You're going to have a good time at Fassler Hall, and good food as well.

Fuji Japanese Cuisine & Sushi Bar, 3739 S. Peoria Ave., Brookside District; Tulsa, OK 74105; (918) 794-4448; fujitulsa .com; Japanese/Sushi; $$$. Ask most Tulsa foodies and chefs where they go to get the best sushi, and you're bound to hear one word: Fuji. Back this up with their winning the Best of the Best Awards from *Oklahoma* magazine for 10 years and you've got a winner. They fly their fish in fresh biweekly, use fresh wasabi, and have been serving it up for almost a quarter century. They also have one of the largest selections around of sashimi, sushi, Japanese imported beer, and sake. If you want something from the kitchen menu instead, there are offerings of bento boxes, tempura, and other fabulous fare. Check their website for specials as they usually include a reasonable "Boat" offering for two. Try their Big O Roll, which is stuffed with snow crab, habañero, *masago,* and fried asparagus, among other things. There is a second location in the Woodland Hills/71st Street Corridor District at 8226 E. 71st St., Tulsa, OK 74133; (918) 250-1821.

Full Moon Cafe, 1525 E. 15th St., Cherry Street District, Tulsa, OK 74120; (918) 583-6666; eatfullmoon.com; Cafe; $. This long-standing little cafe on Cherry Street has been a neighborhood hangout for nightlife, music, and fun for over 20 years. With their outdoor deck patio and their famous tortilla soup, folks love to just gather and gab at Full Moon Cafe. The menu offers up mostly burgers and sandwich fare, but on Saturday or Sunday they are hugely popular for breakfast and brunch items as well. Weekends you can listen to the Dueling Piano Show while you dine, and there are other local musical guests from Tuesday through Thursday. Crowds gather on their Thrifty Thursdays for $4 burgers and on the Friday of the full moon, the restaurant has a party with drink specials. Try their ever-popular and trademarked Chicken Margarita, a grilled chicken breast basted in margarita butter and topped with cheese. If late night is your thing, they offer a "Moonlite Menu" to please as well.

Go West Restaurant and Saloon, 6205 New Sapulpa Rd., West Tulsa, Tulsa, OK 74131; (918) 446-7546; gowestrestaurant .com; Steaks/Southwest/Seafood; $$. Contemporary cowboy cuisine describes the fare at Go West. The eatery is set apart from mainstream Tulsa, but just look for the giant silos sporting the name; it's the way owners Johnny and Aila Wimpy like it. Decorated in classy Western, you'll find some hearty but delicious recipes offered up by Chef John McEachern at this upscale ranch restaurant, like their BBQ scallops and cheese grits with green chile broth, or their **Buffalo Meat Loaf** (see recipe on p. 262). Everything is made fresh with many local ingredients from their ketchup to their steak sauce. There are plenty of other menu offerings like steaks, burgers, and even quail on the menu. After dinner, have a drink at their saloon and bar or dine outside on their 40-seat patio. Even their cocktails have a cowboy theme—try the Purple Cowboy or the Masked Rider when you visit. If you're fortunate enough to dine when the infamous "Slim" is there, make sure you ask to see him!

Hey Mambo, 114 N. Boston Ave., Brady Arts District, Tulsa, OK 74103; (918) 508-7000; heymambo.com; Italian/Pizza; $$. After working in the pizza business for years and developing a love for it, owner Scott Moore finally fulfilled his wish to open his own restaurant and built it to his liking. When you see a New York–style wood-burning pizza oven the likes of which Hey Mambo has, you had better darn well order one of their pies. But Chef Kurt Fichtenberg's menu has a diverse set of items that cause one to want to wander away from the pizza as well, from a rosemary-braised lamb shank to *pollo bracciola* (stuffed chicken breast). Start your meal off with the *dattero scialle,* a plate of five medjool dates stuffed with goat cheese, wrapped in prosciutto, and drizzled with warm honey and thick balsamic vinegar. The prize at the end of your meal is the house-made seasonal gelato in delicious flavors like cinnamon and pumpkin.

Hibiscus Caribbean Bar and Grill, 3316 S. Peoria Ave., Brookside District, Tulsa, OK 74105; (918) 749-4700; hibiscusbrook side.com; Caribbean; $$. This little dive in Brookside is a bar that offers some amazingly good Caribbean cuisine. I suggest ordering some of their delicious hibiscus tea as it will soothe your mouth for what's coming next: spice, and a lot of it. Whipped up by chefs native to Jamaica, the West Indian menu is dominated by dishes with the term "jerk" in them; therefore you can't leave Hibiscus without trying the jerk chicken, swimming in the sweet, spicy, and sour sauce that will make you want to eat it by the spoonful. Snack on the salt cod fish fritters dipped in the jerk sauce on Thursday and watch live salsa dancing, or on the weekend feast on a Rasta Salad while you listen to a live DJ playing reggae. Ingredients are organic and healthy and there is also a selection of vegan dishes that tempt even the meat eaters. Make sure you sample some of the house rum punch or sip on ginger beer or Ting, a grapefruit-based Jamaican carbonated soda.

James E. McNellie's Public House, 409 E. 1st St., Downtown, Tulsa, OK 74120; (918) 382-7468; mcnellies.com; Pub Food; $$. McNellie's Public House is the first of Elliott Nelson's many ventures into the Tulsa dining scene and is known as the place where the in-crowd loves to hang out. Being known as the largest Guinness distributor in the state can only mean one thing . . . great pub food! Because nothing goes better with a good drink than items like fried pickle chips, a kicked-up rendition of classic Irish potato leek soup, or a Landlord's Cottage Pie. While not totally Irish, McNellie's has one of the best hamburgers in town as well, and make sure you ask to substitute sweet potato fries for their regular fries as they are Tulsa favorites.

You may need a while to decide on your beverage of choice, with 350 beer, ale, and cider offerings on tap or in bottles, including locally brewed Marshall beer.

Joe Momma's, 112 S. Elgin Ave., Blue Dome District, Tulsa, OK 74120; (918) 794-6563; joemommas.com; Pizza/Sandwiches; $$. If you happen to be walking down Elgin Avenue, you might be drawn to a storefront reminiscent of an old-school theater. But it wouldn't be the marquee over the window drawing you in. It would be the pizza makers you could see through the windows hand tossing pizza amid a hip, vibrant setting. That would be Joe Momma's. Blake Ewing, the owner, loves to support Tulsa and anything local, and you will find he and Joe Momma's, in turn, have a loyal Tulsa following. There is a stage for live music and events that also doubles as a giant (pull-down) screen for sports viewing. The brick-oven pizza, like the Betty White, is a local favorite and has Alfredo sauce, fresh mozzarella, feta, and Roma tomatoes. However, you can also get baked pastas from a set menu or build your own from a list of pasta, sauces, meats, and toppings. The Orpheum is one of those desserts you secretly love as it's a half-baked skillet cookie topped with ice cream, chocolate sauce, and whipped cream.

Juniper Restaurant & Martini Lounge, 324 E. 3rd St., Downtown District, Tulsa, OK 74120; (918) 794-1090; junipertulsa

.com; Farm to Table; $$$. Chef Justin Thompson, after his stint as executive chef at the widely acclaimed Brasserie and Sonoma restaurants, hand-built this new farm-to-table restaurant himself along with his father. The pride in perfection continues all through the food and drink he serves at Juniper. From house-infused liquors to locally sourced produce, cheese, and meat, what's in season dictates the changing menu that also boasts palate-pleasing European influences. My suggestion? Order the Natural Farms maple-glazed pork belly for starters and then move on to the panéed Tahlequah free-range chicken with polenta, and brussels sprout slaw. For dessert? I'd go for whatever the seasonal cobbler for two is at the moment. It won't disappoint!

KEO, 3524 S. Peoria Ave., Brookside District, Tulsa, OK 74105; (918) 794-8200; keorestaurant.com; Vietnamese/Thai/Asian; $$. Modern Asian sophistication meets wonderful old family Asian tradition at this lovely restaurant in Brookside. Zahidah and Bill Hyman are the owners of KEO, which is named after Zahidah's maiden name. Both worked in the corporate world and decided that suits and ties were getting tiring. They loved many of the Asian places in Tulsa, but decided the city needed an upscale Asian eatery where you could get a cocktail along with your *pho*. Thus KEO was born. Zahidah uses recipes influenced by Vietnamese, Cambodian, Malaysian, and Thai cuisine, and incorporates fresh, local ingredients into her dishes. Complimentary edamame comes out sprinkled with garlic and chiles. The look and feel of the restaurant, with its tall ceilings, amber awnings, pristine cushioned booths, and a white-bricked bar, will put you at ease while you sample Zahidah's version of a Vietnamese crepe, a palate pleaser of stir-fried duck or shrimp and bean sprouts in a lovely sauce and wrapped in a turmeric crepe (see recipe on p. 256). The pair opens a new location in south Tulsa, located in the Tuscana on Yale retail development at 8809 S. Yale, Tulsa, OK 74137, in late fall 2012.

Kilkenny's Irish Pub & Eatery, 1413 E. 15th St., Cherry Street District, Tulsa, OK 74120; (918) 582-8282; tulsairishpub.com; Pub Food; $$. Owner Brett Rehorn had a dream to open an authentic Irish pub and has all but done so with Kilkenny's. You will seriously feel like you're overseas, with patrons knocking back a few pints of Guinness at the bar. No fancy Americanized would-be pub fare here, you'll find only the classics: oysters on the half shell, fish-and-chips, thick, tender corned beef, and my favorite dessert in the world—sticky toffee pudding. Try the delicious Butter Slip Burger, a half pound of ground beef goodness. Of course it wouldn't be a true pub without a major drink list, and Kilkenny's has beer and then some with choices of German, English, and Irish beer and cider and an abundance of Irish whiskeys and single-malt scotch as well. Saturday and Sunday they serve a fantastic brunch including a Breakfast Boxty of eggs, Irish bacon, bangers, and Irish cheddar.

La Hacienda, 4518 S. Peoria Ave., Brookside District, Tulsa, OK 74105; (918) 712-8645; Mexican; $$. La Hacienda is a casual and authentic Mexican restaurant where the food, like slow-simmered carnitas and carne asada, is served on generous platters. When you order, I recommend anything off of the Mexican Favorites section of the menu. It's like down-home cooking would be in a family home in Mexico. The Los Comprados, featuring grilled steak and shrimp, is fantastic, spicy, and just plain delicious. If you're craving real tamales, *tortas,* and gorditas, this just might be the little find you'll love to know about. They also make a mean Mexican breakfast like chorizo eggs. Go on the weekend and try one of their spicy brunch offerings.

Leon's, 3301 S. Peoria Ave., Brookside District, Tulsa, OK 74105; (918) 933-5366; eatatleons.com; Cafe; $$. Leon's is kind of a jack-of-all-trades. You can eat here, or you can drink here, or you can do both. Want to take your family? There's a separate dining room for that as well. The sports-themed eatery has over 19 big-screen TVs so you're bound to find whatever game you're looking to catch, and they always offer discounted pitchers of beer during NFL games. Check their website for some of the specials offered nightly, like their tacos on Tuesday for $1. The menu is a colorful assortment of surprises like the corned beef egg rolls or their KC-Style Burger with peanut butter, bacon, and cheddar cheese. They have all the game food you could want at this hangout, including hero sandwiches and sliders, so drop by and catch a game and some great food.

Local Table, 4329 S. Peoria Ave., Brookside District, Tulsa, OK 74105; (918) 794-8013; localtablerestaurant.com; Farm to Table; $$.

This is another of Chef Tuck Curren's (of Biga Italian, just down the sidewalk) restaurants and just like Biga, he creates some seriously delicious food. There are two big draws to Local Table, one being their Sunday evening wine and appetizer specials, and the other being their 3-course meal for $20. Local is also known for sourcing as much as possible sustainably and locally, so the menu will change according to what's available. Appetizers may vary from a confit of pork belly with winter compote to spicy Korean chicken wings. Entrees are memorable when you consider dishes like Mexican poblano, spinach and black bean lasagna with goat cheese. There is also a Meatless Monday, menu even though there are always vegetarian options on the regular menu as well!

Lucky's Restaurant, 1536 E. 15th St., Cherry Street District, Tulsa, OK 74120; (918) 592-5825; luckysrestauranttulsa.com; American/Farm to Table; $$$$. Talk for a few minutes with Chef Matt Kelley and you will quickly see his passion for local ingredients. You will taste it in Lucky's cuisine, even right down to the pecan wood–smoked meats that serve as a restaurant staple. He and wife Kelley operate this fantastic must-try place in the Cherry Street district and one visit will make you understand why the local crowd loves Lucky's. From their impressive wine list to the farm-to-table food to the romantic atmosphere, you can go to Lucky's for a drink or a feast and feel right at home. For starters try the crispy flatbread with figs, goat cheese and pear, drizzled with white truffle oil and sprinkled with whole fried sage leaves. Lucky's prize dinner features an Asian pork chop that'll make you come back time and time again for more. And for dessert? Don't miss out on the key lime coconut cake. (See Chef Kelley's recipe for **Chicken Pesto Pasta** on p. 258.)

Mod's Crepes, 507 S. Boston Ave., Downtown District, Tulsa, OK 74103; (918) 582-6637; modscrepes.com; French; $. From behind a glass window, owner Rusty Rowe lets you watch him and his staff whip up a variety of sweet and savory crepes on Mod's authentic French crepe griddles. Watch them expertly twirl the thin batter around to perfection and then top it with a wide variety of ingredients, like spinach and artichoke 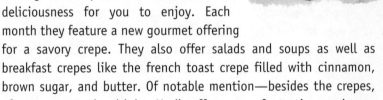 with three cheeses or chocolate-covered strawberries and cream, before neatly folding them up into little bundles of deliciousness for you to enjoy. Each month they feature a new gourmet offering for a savory crepe. They also offer salads and soups as well as breakfast crepes like the french toast crepe filled with cinnamon, brown sugar, and butter. Of notable mention—besides the crepes, of course—are the drinks. Mod's offers some fantastic americano, lattes, and chai, as well as cold drinks like gelato milkshakes and Italian sodas.

My Thai, 3023 S. Harvard Ave., Ste. C, Dowtown District, Tulsa, OK 74114; (918) 794-7093; Thai; $. Noot Jiniaseranee began working with her parents years ago in the kitchen of their now-closed restaurant. She also attended cooking school in Thailand.

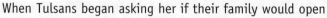

When Tulsans began asking her if their family would open another restaurant, Noot obliged by opening what locals simply call "My Thai." Her cuisine brings rave reviews from all who dine there. Try any of the curries as they are all delicious, but the green curry might be the standout. The Drunken Noodles are pungently rich and spicy and wonderful and the steamed fish in Thai herbs will leave you feeling healthy and light but without feeling like you've missed out on anything. The dining room is small, so you should get there early to get a seat.

Palace Cafe, 1301 E. 15th St., Cherry Street District, Tulsa, OK 74120; (918) 582-4321; palacetulsa.com; Farm to Table; $$$. Owner and Chef James Shrader is a graduate of the Culinary Institute of America and could be described as a culinary genius. That's because his loyal following of locals love his creative culinary offerings like his bento menu. At mere pennies per portion, you can order one or a half dozen of these small plates like a salmon cake or a mini filet mignon. Using as many local ingredients as possible, Palace Cafe has a decidedly Asian flair on American food with menu offerings such as five-spice crispy duck and shrimp shiitake pot stickers, but also features delicious American dinner items as well like wood-grilled tenderloin with wild mushrooms and lobster ravioli. A recently added and renovated bar and lounge add cozy comfort for your sipping and snacking pleasure as well.

Queenie's Plus, 1834 Utica Sq., Utica Square District, Tulsa, OK 74114; (918) 749-3481; queeniesoftulsa.com; Bakery/Breakfast/ Sandwiches; $. This quaint little cafe is in the center of Utica Square and is surrounded by upscale shopping. Ruth Young opened this place over 28 years ago and it is still a favorite among diners (and shoppers, naturally). They bake all of their pastries, cakes, and breads using all fresh ingredients. Young and company also use local grass-fed chicken and eggs and all-natural beef in their more savory dishes. The coffee Queenie's serves up is locally roasted Topeca coffee, so sip on the outdoor sidewalk patio in their bright pink and orange chairs, or head inside to the cozy dining area. Queenie's is a favorite with locals for their breakfast, but they also serve lunch and dinner dishes. Their specialty is their "famous grilled cheese sandwiches" and their chicken salad is beloved by all. And as far as sweets go? The strawberry cream cake is the star, but I am pretty partial to the lemon bars, which are among the best I've ever had.

Smoke, On Cherry Street, 1542 E. 15th St., Cherry Street District, Tulsa, OK 74120; (918) 949-4440; smoketulsa.com; Farm to Table/Steaks/Seafood; $$$. Under the careful watch of Executive Chef Erick Reynolds, Smoke is a truly unique place to dine. Its name can take on two meanings, from the meats that are house smoked to the restaurant's lounge, complete with humidor, wood-paneled walls and leather couches and chairs. The menu is creatively smoky from the grilled romaine Caesar salad to a bevy of meats like quail, steaks, and bacon. The restaurant incorporates many local ingredients, from meat to produce, in their meals. Visit them on the weekend for live jazz music. Smoke also serves brunch on the weekend and offers up dishes like chicken-fried bacon and waffles. Put a creative spin on a night out and take Smoke's Culinary Safari, a cooking class with five other couples where the chefs teach everyone how to prepare a 6-course meal.

Sonoma Bistro & Wine Bar, 3523 S. Peoria Ave., Tulsa, OK 74105; (918) 747-9463; sonomatulsa.com; Wine Bar; $$. **Tim Baker** was inspired when traveling on the west coast through the vineyards and eateries in Northern California. He dreamed of opening a simple bistro restaurant using quality fresh ingredients that offered cuisine paired with a wonderful selection of over 100 wines. He is living his dream in Sonoma Bistro & Wine Bar. All wines are available by the glass and the food is organic and wonderful. Start off with the fruit and cheese plate, which varies frequently and could include fruit, nuts, cheeses, spreads, and toast wedges (if you go during one of their happy hours, you can get it for half off!). Executive Chef Nona Heklmick offers temptations like roasted corn soup with smoked cheddar shortbread to start your meal out deliciously. For lunch try the pepperoni grilled cheese sandwich and tomato bisque and for dinner, try the citrus and garlic chicken and finish the evening off with one of those wonderful wines and some Blueberry Gooey Butter Cake.

Stonehorse Cafe, 1748 Utica Sq., Utica Square District, Tulsa, OK 74114; stonehorsecafe.com; Farm to Table; $$$. **Sleek, modern,**

casual, and comfortable, with amazingly great food could be the perfect description for Stonehorse Cafe. Chef Tim Inman and his wife Lise have created a culinary gem with the Stonehorse Cafe. Just ask any local Tulsan. With an ever-changing menu depending on what is local and fresh, Chef Tim's inspiration goes back to his roots of living on a dairy farm in New York and is seen in his famous Truck Stop–Style Meat Loaf. Dishes of delicious American classics can show some classic French influence, as seen in creations like his mustard-crusted rack of lamb. The restaurant has an excellent wine menu as well as a fabulous cocktail and beer list. You'll also want to make a point to visit the market in the back for some fabulous gourmet takeout meats and products. Reservations are highly recommended—this place can fill up fast, and for good reason.

The Sushi Place, 115 W. 3rd St., Downtown District, Tulsa, OK 74103; (918)-574-8518; sushiplaceonline.com; Sushi; $$. Joey Leong and Jaymie Tan own and operate this little hidden treasure and have built it from the ground up. When they first opened The Sushi Place, they did so with five tables and empty walls and turned it into a cozy and friendly little eatery. Jaymie will be happy to tell you about their dishes and her infectious smile will light up with passion as she describes their 30-plus sushi rolls, specials, and other offerings. The miso soup is made from scratch and is some of the best I've had. I really enjoyed the ginger-rich *ika* salad (calamari). The sushi is very good and fresh with traditional and some not-so traditional offerings. Sushi purists will enjoy the raw spicy tuna and the traditional rolls and *nigiri,* but venture on the wild side and try the 918 rolls (Tulsa's area code) or indulge in the Cheesy Maki Roll with its cheese-baked shrimp on top. The Sushi Place also has a quaint selection of sakes, like plum, *ume, nigori,* and Champagne sake, and also some imported and domestic beer as well. I've always found the best sushi places to be those smaller, welcoming holes in the wall, and The Sushi Place is one of those places.

Te Kei's, 1616 S. Utica Ave., Utica Square District, Tulsa, OK 74104; (918) 382-7777; tekeis.com; Asian Fusion; $$. This eatery's name literally means "special guest" and that is what the motto is at Te Kei's. Dine surrounded by richly paneled carved wooden walls (brought from a palace in Indonesia) decorated with artifacts from all over Thailand, Japan, and China. The food you'll see on the menu reflects the same philosophy as the artifacts, as it originates from varying Asian influences such as Korea, Malaysia, Japan, and Thailand. Menu items range from Korean tacos to noodle bowls to delectable and spicy Asian spareribs and they also offer a gluten-free menu as well.

Tucci's Cafe Italia, 1344 E. 15th St., Cherry Street District, Tulsa, OK 74120; (918) 582-3456; Italian; $$$. In business for almost 20 years, Tucci's is a certifiable Tulsa classic. This little cozy Italian eatery began as a pizza-by-the-slice stop for folks on Cherry Street, but has now evolved into an upscale delicious lunch and dinner favorite instead. The mother-and-son team of Doris, Marc, and

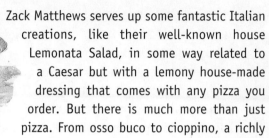

Zack Matthews serves up some fantastic Italian creations, like their well-known house Lemonata Salad, in some way related to a Caesar but with a lemony house-made dressing that comes with any pizza you order. But there is much more than just pizza. From osso buco to cioppino, a richly brothed and delicious seafood stew, you can sit in a dimly lit and romantic setting at Tucci's and feel like you're in old Hollywood glamour. For dessert, try a gelato or the triple chocolate cake with a glass of wine and if the weather is nice, dine on the curtained patio and take in the sounds of Cherry Street.

The White Owl, 1325 E. 15th St., Cherry Street District, Tulsa, OK 74120; (918) 933-5050; whiteowloncherry.com; Pub Food; $$. Chef Curt Herrmann left Tulsa for Spain and London for almost ten years. While there, he picked up a love and a knack for pub fare and upon his return to Tulsa, he signed up with owners Jason Hunt and his wife Kelly Finegan Hunt to open this Cherry Street pub. Wood bar tops and metal barstools line the room where the pub fare served up might not be the typical English pub food you're thinking of. There are offerings like carne asada nachos, and the must-try fried zucchini strips with homemade ranch dressing. Every pub has to have fish-and-chips, and The White Owl is no exception. They come out hot and crispy and are served not only with tartar sauce but malt vinegar as well. And it wouldn't be a pub without beer. White Owl offers over 10 choices on tap and a full bar as well.

Wild Fork, 1820 Utica Square Ave., Utica Square District, Tulsa, OK 74114; (918) 742-0712; wildfork.com; Steaks/Seafood/Breakfast; $$$. Tucked away on a corner in Utica Square, Wild Fork is one of those places you want to go on a special Saturday afternoon. Or anytime for that matter. Their covered patio complete with stemware and classy tables will beckon you to sit outside, dine alfresco, and sip a Pyrat Island Punch. The Wild Fork's owners, Julie Woolman and Kim Michie, opened the restaurant 17 years ago. Julie is a trained chef and Kim bakes the pastries using her family recipes like toasted coconut vanilla bean custard pie. From breakfast to dinner, the food is fabulous at this eatery. The sherry tomato soup and house bread was a rotating special, but the local demand for it was so great it is now a staple on the menu. The grilled chicken sandwich is housed in an incredible flatbread and is fantastic. They have a nice wine menu that features house wines in 5-ounce, 8.5-ounce, and 3-ounce petite pours, as well as bottles and sparkling wines and Champagne.

Yokozuna, 309 E. 2nd St., Blue Dome District, Tulsa, OK 74120; (918) 508-7676; yokozunatulsa.com; Asian Fusion/Sushi; $$. Yokozuna's look and atmosphere are an eclectic mix of brick walls, steel beams, high ceilings, and retro lighting combined with a hip sushi bar and an even longer bar counter that wraps around almost the entire restaurant. Located in the heart of the Blue Dome District, you'll see a very fun young and trendy crowd in Yokozuna. This eatery has a mix of sushi prepared by Master sushi chef Jin Baek and Asian fusion such as pad thai or chicken chile ramen. Sit around their hinoki wood bar (a prized Japanese cypress) and sample an Asian-inspired cocktail or try their extensive sake and wine list. Try the Roll and Gift, a tempura shrimp, jalapeño, and chipotle cream cheese roll or their pork belly ramen with a quail egg on top.

Landmarks

The Chalkboard, 1324 S. Main St., Terwilleger Heights, Tulsa, OK 74119; (918) 582-1964; thechalkboard-tulsa.com; Bistro/Cafe Fare; $$$. When I see "Artisan Cheese Board" on a menu, I know I'm going to love the eatery. And The Chalkboard has a great one complete with garlic confit, fruit, and dried preserves. Look for many fresh organic salads on their menu. But that's just for starters at one of Tulsa's long-standing and superb eateries located inside the historic Hotel Ambassador on the lower level. I love that they serve entrees like old-fashioned beef Wellington in a classy, warm, and glowing ambience. You'll understand why they are continually picked for Best of the Best by *Oklahoma* magazine for various awards like Best Continental Menu, Best Gourmet Dining, and Best Wine List, and received a People's Choice award for their signature white chocolate bread pudding. During nice weather, sit on their charming patio and take in the views of Terwilleger Heights. Brunch at the Chalkboard is fabulous with wonderful menu items like a blackened filet Southwest eggs Benedict and live music on Sunday featuring a jazz theme. Reservations are highly recommended.

Claud's Hamburgers, 3834 S. Peoria Ave., Brookside District, Tulsa, OK 74105; (918) 742-8332; Burgers; $. Find the small white building located away from street-front Peoria Avenue, and you've found a diamond in the rough, my friends. Open since 1954, Claud's has been frying up onion burgers for over 50 years the same way. They smash them onto a flat griddle with some chopped onions, top them with American cheese and serve them with some great hand-cut french fries or homemade coleslaw. If you choose to dine in, you can sit to the left side of the restaurant and watch this process or you can take your order to go. Space is limited, so you may opt to do takeout, but either way, when you bite into one of these simple masterpieces you'll sigh with joy. Order the double meat burger if you have a hearty appetite and get two caramelized patties stacked together.

Coney I-Lander, 3919 S. Peoria Ave., Brookside District, Tulsa, OK 74105; (918) 742-7259; Hot Dogs; $. Sometimes basic is the best when it comes to a hot dog. Started by the Economou family after Christ Economou ended up in Oklahoma following stints in Dallas and Houston in 1926, Coney I-Lander has been a Tulsa tradition for what seems like forever. Back then, you would order a dog and sit at old school desks while waiting for your food to come out. Today they boast seven locations around the Tulsa area and still crank out the same flat-top griddled hot dogs nestled in a steamed hot dog bun and served up with some chili, onions, and a little mustard and paprika. The Greek-style chili is finely ground and the hot dogs come simply with a side of chips and a drink. Not expected, however, are the other offerings at Coney I-Lander: tamales, served on the small side, and spaghetti topped with the same delicious Greek chili.

Eddy's Steakhouse, 3510 E 31st St., Midtown District, Tulsa, OK 74135; (918) 742-5212; eddysoftulsa.com; Lebanese Steak House; $$. If you've never been to a Lebanese steak house, let me clue you in. Eddy's had a related steak house in Oklahoma City that has now closed but this dark and swanky Tulsa landmark (since 1956) is still going strong. Lebanese hors d'oeuvres are a little bit different and such is the case at Eddy's Steakhouse. You're going to receive a plate of carrots, celery, and the like along with some hummus, tabouleh, and crackers to start things out. I love the combination of the hummus and tabouleh on the crackers, but then the wonderful, aromatic cabbage roll arrives, stuffed with ground beef, rice, and cinnamon-scented goodness. Follow that up with salad and rolls, and you're ready for your entree. And I suggest a steak—specifically the Eddy's rib eye club steak, which is downright delicious and presented with a simple baked potato. For dessert, try the one and only Turtle Cheesecake to wind down your evening.

Elmer's BBQ, 4130 S. Peoria Ave., Brookside District, Tulsa, OK 74105; (918) 742-6702; Barbecue; $$. Walking into Elmer's, you may notice the giant sign over the door boasting "It Be Bad!" It isn't so bad folks, it's good. Elmer's has been pleasing Tulsans with their barbecue for over 20 years. Inside of this retro diner, Elmer's, like any decent barbecue place, serves up smoky and fall-off-the-bone ribs, sausages, hot links, chopped pork, bologna, and beef. Their "Famous Badwich" is a crazy piling up of several of their meats onto one bun. Meat is smoked simply here to let its natural flavor shine through. Want to sample it all? Try the Nelson Sampler and get all four meats plus sides like the green beans with bits of their smoky ribs cooked right into them. See why former President Bill Clinton personally thanked the restaurant for feeding him when he passed through Tulsa, and grab some stick-to-your-ribs grub at Elmer's.

Lambrusco'z to Go, 1344 E. 41st St. Brookside District, Tulsa, OK 74105; (918) 496-1246; lambruscoz.com; Deli; $. For over 25 years, Lambrusco'z has been a deli staple in Tulsa. If you're a vegetable and side-dish lover like me, you'll be thrilled with the choices offered behind the dining area in the glass cases. The way it works at Lambrusco'z is that you pick your meal out of the glass cases, where you'll find everything from the delectable Boar's Head meats and cheeses for sandwiches to entrees like grilled salmon or soups like rosemary bean soup. Don't even get me started on the side dishes like homemade mac and cheese or sautéed brussels sprouts. But I caution you that you absolutely should not walk out of Lambrusco'z without trying one of their famous cookies, baked daily. In fact, you can't go wrong with any of their baked treat selections to nicely round out your meal.

Weber's Root Beer Stand, 3817 S. Peoria Ave., Brookside District, Tulsa, OK 74105; webersoftulsa.com; Burgers; $. Boasting the oldest operating neon sign in Tulsa (since 1933), Weber's was the starting point of eating out in the Brookside District. In the late 1800s, Oscar Weber Bilby home brewed his recipe for root beer that consisted of 14 natural ingredients, fire brewed and aged in birch bark barrels. Years later, Oscar's grandson Rick Bilby and his wife Jennifer still own and operate this original store on Peoria. They still serve the same 14-ingredient recipe for the homemade root beer and some fantastic grilled hamburgers to go with it. The burgers are made with 100 percent fresh ground Angus beef. The root beer is served in ice-cold frosted mugs and to go along with the burgers, order up some of their wonderful, crispy french fries and onion rings (some of the best around!) to make your meal complete.

Specialty Stores, Markets & Producers

Ann's Bakery, 7 N. Harvard Ave., Tulsa, OK 74115; (918) 834-2345; annsbakery.com. Around since pre-World War II days (1938), Ann's boasts of being the oldest "from scratch" bakery in Tulsa.

Ann opened and operated the bakery out of her house. Now in its third generation of baking with Shannon Harris, Ann's offers all sorts of baked goods, from wedding cakes to cinnamon rolls to cookies. The sausage rolls are famous and scrumptious as are any of their quick breads like pumpkin or blueberry, and don't even get me started on their pastries and doughnuts. One of their cheese danishes is enough to make a grown man cry, with its mound of cream cheese filling in the center. Ann's also serves up local Topeca coffee, which nicely complements any baked treat you may desire.

Cafe Cubana, 1328 E. 15th St., Cherry Street District, Tulsa, OK 74120; (918) 584-2233; facebook.com/pages/Cafe-Cubana. **Cafe** Cubana knows how to serve up a good espresso or cappuccino with the proper crema and foam along with some truly good grounds. James George, the owner of Cafe Cubana also has another love in cigars; therefore his other business venture is Fogue & Bates Tobacco. Of course he offers a humidor cabinet at his coffee house as well. How's that for diversity? At the Cubana, you can get a smoothie, a nice hot tea, or most importantly, a great cup of joe. To accompany your steaming or iced coffee, order up a biscotti, muffin, or even a bowl of steaming hot oatmeal.

Cafe Topeca Coffee Shop, 115 W. 5th St., Ste. 169, Downtown, Tulsa, OK 74103; (918) 592-9090; topecacoffee.com. **Get a cup** of java at many restaurants, cafes, and bistros in town and you may just see the phrase "proudly brewed Topeca Coffee" on the menu. That's because locally roasted Topeca Coffee is somewhat revered around these parts, and with good reason. Owners John and Margarita continue to run this family-owned business that's been around since 1870. Margarita's brother runs the operation where the beans are grown in the hills of El Salvador and the beans are shipped back home and ground in their local roaster in Tulsa. Inside the Mayo Hotel downtown, John and Margarita now operate the Cafe Topeca Coffee Shop. Sit in Southwest flair and sip a heady cup of their delicious coffee and enjoy one of their cinnamon rolls.

Cherry Street Farmers' Market, Located all along 15th Street corridor, Cherry Street District, Tulsa, OK; cherrystreetfarmers market.com. The Cherry Street Farmers' Market is the oldest running Tulsa market and the go-to for Tulsa area farmers to exhibit their colorful gems of produce and product. Visit the largest of Tulsa's farmers' markets on Sat from 7 to 11 a.m. from Apr to Oct and you will find a plethora of locally grown lusciousness, from carrots to tomatoes to herbs. But produce is not all you'll find. Like to buy local? You can even get meats, cheeses, dairy, and the breads here as well. And when the farmers' market is open, all the eateries roll out their finest specials. There is also live music, so going to the farmers' market on Cherry Street is a multifaceted experience you won't want to miss. Be sure to set your alarm though, because most of the good stuff sells out early! The Cherry Street now also offers a second market in the Brookside District on Wednesday from Apr through Sept, from 8 a.m. to 12 p.m., located in the northeast corner of 41st and Peoria in the parking lot of the Food Pyramid store.

Coffee House on Cherry Street, 1502 E. 15th St., Cherry Street District, Tulsa, OK 74120; (918) 779-6137; thecoffeehouseoncherry street.com. Charmingly quaint, The Coffee House on Cherry Street is always packed with locals hanging out while drinking field-to-cup locally roasted Topeca coffee. One fantastic offering other than the coffee at this place is the glass case inside the door that houses everything from pastries and cookies to more savory offerings like quiche or quesadillas. You might see a bread pudding with icing dripping down the side of the cappuccino cup it's been baked in. There are various seating groupings and levels where couches or tables and chairs offer relaxation among friends. The decor is colorful and after entering the coffee shop, you can find your way out to the truly wonderful little patio where you can take your bottomless coffee (for $3) and sip it along with your friends.

La Donna's Fancy Foods, 1615 E. 15th St., Cherry Street District, Tulsa, OK 74120; (918) 582-1523; ladonnasonline.com. Named for its owner, La Donna Cullinan, this gourmet food shop is a little gem tucked away on Cherry Street where you can find some amazing things to take home to your kitchen, from cheese to housewares to pasta to my favorite . . . chocolate. She has an entire wall dedicated to "Made in Oklahoma" products that you can sample along with famous, locally made pottery. The star at La Donna's in my opinion is the cheese selection. Note the giant white board behind the cheese cooler when you walk in and you'll see that she can get you just about anything you want in the way of delicious cheese. She also carries coveted chocolates like Askinosie and Vosges. There are also imported pastas, sauces, olives oils, and just about any other gourmet food item you could wish for. La Donna will make you up a charming gift basket if you desire so stop on in to take some stuff to go!

Mecca Coffee, 1143 E. 33rd Place, Brookside District, Tulsa, OK 74105; (918) 749-3509; meccacoffee.com. Mecca Coffee Company has been around since 1921, roasting coffee and grinding spices, which is how they got their start. Ninety-plus years later, their still-thriving store has expanded into a mecca of gourmet kitchen goods. Here you can still find great coffee and spices, but also a bevy of other things like home-brew beer or winemaking needs, cookware, tableware, and tons of gourmet products. They offer an extra-virgin olive oil bar with 26 high-quality olive oils from around the world as well as numerous offerings of white and dark balsamic vinegars. This would be a wonderful place to buy a gift for your gourmet or wine connoisseur friend as they offer beautiful stemware and a large line of gourmet food items. And for that fella in your life? They have a humidor full of top-of-the-line cigars, so stop in and you'll find something for everyone.

The Pearl Farmers' Market, Brookside District, Tulsa, OK (corner of 6th and Peoria Ave. in Centennial Park); pearlfarmers market.com. This farmers' market is open Apr through Sept and is open in the evening from 4:30 to 7 p.m. Fresh, locally grown, and mostly organic vegetables and flowers along with meats and much more await you at this market. Usually a local band will be playing and a true sense of community abounds with families, dogs, and children out and about. Pearl Farmers' Market also offers farm-to-table recipes on their site as well.

Petty's Fine Foods, 1964 Utica Sq., Utica Square District, Tulsa, OK 74152; (918) 747-8616; pettysfinefoods.com. Petty's Fine Foods has been a Tulsa staple since its opening in 1945 by L. G. Rowan and Robert D. Petty. The owners had a dream to start a food store offering up the highest quality and best service available to Tulsans. At Petty's you might find those hard sought after ethnic and imported products you can't find in your regular market. You can also find USDA choice and prime aged beef. They offer a New York–style delicatessen providing customers with a large variety of cheeses, meats, salads, and their Gourmet Express entrees. Don't want to make the trip? Petty's delivers and they also have a fine catering department as well. Their bakery offers fresh baked European-style breads and pastries and there are always delicious cookies and cakes. Their gift shop will also put together anything from a basket of their wonderful fruit to boxes of their fantastic steaks.

Shades of Brown Coffee & Art, 3302 S. Peoria Ave., Brookside District, Tulsa, OK 74105; (918) 747-3000; shadesofbrowncoffee .com. Eclectic, mismatched furniture sits on the patio for college students and the like to hang out and, I'm sure, discuss their philosophy of life. It has remained my go-to place when I visit Tulsa as I love their coffee, macchiatto, and chai latte. I am also a big fan of the pottery coffee mugs they sell with their logo engraved on them by local Linda Coward. The coffee is fantastic and in generous portions and you can request it in one of those fabulous pottery mugs. To accompany your beverage, pick from an assortment of baked goods made fresh daily like kugelhopfs, scones, muffins, cookies, or even cheesecake. Like any good coffee shop, Shades offers a Jazz Monday and welcomes local musicians on Friday and Saturday evening.

East & North Tulsa

East Tulsa is roughly located between Admiral and 21st Street and extends out to Mingo. There are many outdoor events in this area due to a major park, Redbud Nature Preserve, and an athletic facility located within its limits. Some call it the hospitality corridor as it houses many hotels. Perhaps most exciting for the food scene is that it hosts a large section of Historic Route 66, which is known for having great stops along its length for eateries.

The North Tulsa area is perhaps best known for its close proximity to the Tulsa International Airport and Mohawk Park, where you can visit the Tulsa Zoo, the Oxley Nature Center, and the Tulsa Air and Space Museum. It also houses the American Airlines maintenance facility which provides loads of jobs to the Tulsa community. Needless to say, due to an airport, various tourist sites, and a large company, restaurants in this area of town are sure to be fantastic.

Dooley's Angus Inn, 201 S. Main St., Broken Arrow, OK 74012; (918) 258-2333; angusinn.net; Steak House; $$$. Michael Larry Dooley's father owned an Angus cattle ranch when he was growing up. Little did he know at that time he'd one day own a steak house that would earn the title "Broken Arrow's Top Steak House," or be named as one of the top three steak house choices in Oklahoma by the Oklahoma Restaurant Association. True to the eatery's name, Dooley's serves Angus beef and is the only spot in Oklahoma where you can get a Southern-fried rib eye. Start off your meal with a blue crab and shrimp dip served with toasted baguettes and then just try and pick from one of the steaks, like a 32-ounce, bone-in-rib eye, and a center-cut New York strip. Or maybe you'd rather opt for seafood as Dooley's has that as well, with everything from king crab legs to spicy breaded cajun crawfish. Dooley's has a nice wine and imported beer list and you can enjoy a tasty beverage with their 14-layer chocolate cake for dessert.

Dragonmoon Tea Co., 1927 S. Harvard Ave., East Tulsa, Tulsa, OK 74112; (918) 742-8322; facebook.com/dragonmoontea; Cafe Fare; $. In a lovely converted 1920s home lies the Dragonmoon Tea Co. The creation of sisters Sara Creed-Piper and Susan Blair, Dragonmoon makes tea a very serious business and offers over 90 teas and various sandwiches, salads, and sweets to go along with it. Classics like egg salad are on the menu along with other offerings like Calcutta chicken salad, which includes a delightful blend of curry and chutney mixed in for a different flavor. The soups, like their savory tomato Parmesan, are always homemade and superb. And for that sweet tooth? Never fear for upon walking in, you'll notice a glass case full of lusciousness, featuring baked goods such as tartlets, cupcakes, and scones. If available, try the bread pudding, as it's to die for! Visit them for afternoon tea and high tea by checking their website for details; reservations are recommended. Visit the gift shop before you leave and take away some wonderful honeys, jams, and other foodie novelties.

Evelyn's, 3014 N. 74th East Ave., North Tulsa, Tulsa, OK 74115; (918) 835-1212; Southern; $$. She doesn't keep her place open on the weekend, so if you go to Evelyn's make it from Monday through Friday or you'll be out of luck. Wand J. Armstrong is the genius behind the restaurant's addictive, light, and crispy fried chicken that makes people drive from all over the Tulsa area just to wait in line and grab a bite of their own. The diner is named after her mom, who taught her the way around a kitchen. We all sure do love Evelyn, bless her heart! In addition to finger lickin' fried chicken, she also makes a mean pork chop. Choose from comforting down-home side dishes like candied yams or smothered cabbage. For dessert try their peach cobbler or banana pudding, because at $2, they are all you can eat. Wash it all down with a sweet tea to make your Southern experience truly memorable.

The Gnarley Dawg, 6011 S. Mingo Rd., East Tulsa, Tulsa, OK 74146; (918) 893-4663; thegnarleydawg.com; Hot Dogs; $. In mid 2010, something happened in East Tulsa that had people driving over that way just for some food. What happened is that the Rucks family—Don, his wife Susie, and their daughter Traci—acted on Don's dream to open a hot dog place that lets you play dress-up with an entire slew of toppings for their many different options of dogs including all-beef, lean turkey, andouille sausage, bratwurst, and hot links, along with some premium options like chicken sausage and jalapeño cheese sausage. There are also "gnarley sides" like the Gnarley Noodles (mac and cheese) and Gnarley Beans.

Guang Zhou Dim Sum, Expo Square at 4003 E. 11th St., East Tulsa, Tulsa, OK 74112; (918) 835-7888; guangzhoudimsum.com; Dim Sum; $$. Dim sum is served at Guang Zhou on rolling steam carts that are wheeled to your table periodically to allow you to choose one or more of their delicious dishes. After you're given a menu and a long checklist, the carts start coming. Choose from a variety of wonderfully soft dumplings full of various fillings like pork or steamed shrimp; each polished silver steamer dish will contain four of these small gems. I am a huge fan of the lotus leaf sticky rice (*lo mai gai*). There are also sweet offerings of dim sum for the end of your meal; try the pineapple buns with their egg cream filling or a steamed lotus seed bun. The dim sum is served daily from the checklist menu but the carts only roll out on Saturday and Sunday from 10:30 a.m. to 3 p.m. There is a second location at 2115 S. Garnett Rd., Tulsa, OK 74128; (918) 438-8878.

Hmong Cafe, 11197 E. 31st St., East Tulsa, Tulsa, OK 74146; (918) 828-9192; Asian Fusion; $$. The Yang family opened the doors to Hmong Cafe in East Tulsa in 2007 and the food is primarily influenced by Thai, Lao, and Vietnamese cuisine, but yes, there is even a little bit of Chinese mixed in as well. Over 4 years later, this eatery has become one of the favorites in Asian fare and people drive from all over Tulsa to eat there. Choose from varieties of papaya salad, with its fresh crunch and spicy lime dressing, to *lahb* salads, a delicious blending of meat, fresh herbs, bean sprouts, and spices, served room temperature. And of course, there is the big hit at the restaurant, the ever-popular *pho* noodle soup. Whatever you get at Hmong Cafe, you will love the mix of salty, sweet, sour, and hot in all their dishes. You'll find yourself going back to satisfy that craving time and time again.

Korean Garden, 12773 E. 41st St., East Tulsa, Tulsa, OK 74146; (918) 627-9292; Korean; $$. The setting may be unpretentious, nestled in a strip mall and a little unfamiliar to most diners, but the food is delicious and surprisingly wonderful at this little Korean diner. Here, you can get traditional Korean cooked food like bibimbap, a stone bowl rice dish heated in the oven, and topped with numerous crisp vegetables like cucumber, carrots, and also some of their smoky Korean BBQ meat (*bulgogi*). If you'd rather, order off the buffet on the weekends where they serve up a variety of traditional Korean fare like *kalbi* (beef short ribs) with their smoky marinated goodness or try the vegetable maki and kimchee. The *soon* tofu is a pot of bubbling deliciousness with soft tofu and spicy kimchee in the broth. If you're feeling adventurous, try some Korean cuisine at this little gem; you won't regret it.

Margaret's German Restaurant, 5107 S. Sheridan Rd., East Tulsa, Tulsa, OK 74145; (918) 622-3747; margaretsgermanrestaurant.com; German; $$. A pregnant Margaret Rzepczynski and her husband, Andrew, arrived in Tulsa in 1982 with $200 in their pocket and managed to start Margaret's German Restaurant. Lucky for the locals, this restaurant is still thriving today and putting out some tasty food. I am of German descent, and seeing the light rye bread baked at Margaret's made me sit up and take note, as it looked just like my mom's famous German light rye. Featuring some of the best authentic German food in Tulsa outside the huge Oktoberfest celebration, Margaret's menu offers plenty of sausages, sauerkraut, and schnitzel. The variety of sausages includes their widely popular Polish sausage and coarse bratwurst. For lunch, you can get some fabulous sandwiches like liverwurst, schinkenwurst, and pastrami. For dinner, start out with the homemade potato pancakes with applesauce and then move onto sauerbraten, marinated German-style and served in a German sweet-and-sour sauce. The eatery also has a fabulous Black Forest cake, and you can wash it all down with German beer off their extensive beer list.

The Oklahoma Food Co-op

The Oklahoma Food Co-op is really starting to take off in Oklahoma due to the demand for sustainable and local food in the state and the increasing awareness of agroterrorism and its related health risks. The co-op only sells food and non-food products made in Oklahoma, and local folk are starting to realize how important it is to not only support local growers and producers, but that it is better for their families as well. Through the co-op, you can learn exactly whom you're buying from and how they farm or create the product. With the co-op, you know how your produce is grown or how the livestock was raised and fed for your meat. As of 2011, there were roughly 4,000 members, so obviously we still have a ways to go but with over 4,000 items now available to order, we believe the co-op will grow substantially over the next 10 years.

For more information, visit their website at oklahomafood .coop, and follow their Twitter feed, @oklafoodcoop.

Pho Da Cao, 9066 E. 31st St., East Tulsa, Tulsa, OK 74145; (918) 270-2715; wphodacao.webs.com; Pho; $. Some of the best *pho* available in Oklahoma is at Pho Da Cao in Tulsa, and it comes with your choice of a variety of meats and toppings. Are you a *pho* fan? Then try one of the more authentic soups at Pho Da Cao by branching out to the meatballs, tendon, or tripe. If you haven't tried *pho*, start out with the basic P1 with eye of round steak and well-done brisket. At Pho Da Cao, you can also try another magnificent soup—the *bun bo hue,* a rich broth-laden bowl of spiciness, complete with rice noodles and a variety of meats including pork loaf. They also have delicious items like spring rolls and fried pork dumplings that are a great start to the meal.

Shiloh's, 12521 E. 52nd St., East Tulsa, Tulsa, OK 74146; (918) 254-1500; shilohsrestaurant.com; Southern; $. Cooking is in this family's blood. Going on three generations in the restaurant business, Shiloh's carries on Granny Ethel's traditional Southern recipes and offers up some of the best Southern fare around. Shiloh's is a fantastic place to go for a good ol' breakfast done right. You can order anything from unusually large cinnamon rolls to blueberry pancakes and crispy hash browns. The omelets are generous and come with various sides including a choice of their homemade breads toasted up. The entrees are equally home cooked and you can order sandwiches, hamburgers, or hand-breaded and boneless pan-fried chicken. The star of the show is their homemade yeast rolls that are almost as big as the plate. If you're looking for comforting, down-home cooking, this is your place. There is a second location at 2604 N. Aspen Ave., Broken Arrow, OK 74012; (918) 277-4849.

Shish-Kabob's, 11605 E. 31st St., East Tulsa, Tulsa, OK 74146; (918) 663-9383; Mediterranean; $$. Shadi and Sourena Afshari own and operate this fresh and flavorful Middle Eastern eatery after purchasing it from its previous owner. They revamped the menu items to their own liking and it's become a hit among those who love Mediterranean cuisine. The atmosphere is simple, warm, and inviting, but the food is anything but simple. Spiced with layers of flavor, the appetizers are a must-try, from the smoky baba ghanoush, drizzled with minted olive oil, to the *sambusa,* a delightful pastry filled with meat and potatoes. Next you will need to choose from their shish kebabs, and the options are wonderfully seasoned ground meats like lamb, beef, or chicken pressed around skewers and grilled to perfection. They also offer other main fare like gyros and *ghormeh sabzi,* a wonderful mix of spinach, fenugreek leaves, beef, and herbs. For dessert, there is baklava, rose cake, or Persian ice cream, and speaking of Persia, on Wednesday Sourena cooks special Persian dishes not on the regular menu.

Umberto's Pizza, 3228 E. 21st St., East Tulsa, Tulsa, OK 74114; (918) 712-1999; Pizza; $$. This college-style hangout serves up some of the best New York–style pizza pies in town. There are two casual dining rooms with booths and tables, which are needed during their busy lunch rush. Start out with the sausage rolls, which are warm and a little spicy and come with a nice marinara dipping sauce. I am always a sucker for garlic knots, and theirs are truly yummy. The pizza pies come out sliced in eight huge slices. If you don't want a whole pizza, you can also order at Umberto's by the slice and you'll get a thin, crispy, large slice of pizza you'll almost have to fold in half to eat. If you're looking for a casual pizza place, you may just want to head over to Umberto's.

Viet Huong, 7919 E. 21st St., East Tulsa, Tulsa, OK 74129; (918) 664-1682; Vietnamese; $. The Tran family pride themselves on dishing out amazing food. Actually, they turn out amazing Vietnamese food every day at Viet Huong using fresh, quality ingredients that have brought them a loyal following for over 20 years. While the interior may not be fancy, the food is unforgettably authentic Vietnamese deliciousness. Both varieties of spring rolls are a true treat—whether you choose the fresh, abundantly sized spring rolls filled with vegetables or the crispy fried version, you'll crave them after your first visit. Many say their *pho* is the best in Tulsa, but go beyond the *pho* to try the *buns* or the teriyaki chicken. Both will win over your heart. Stay away from the Americanized menu and order off the Vietnamese menu, although I'd be hard pressed to dismiss anything you could get at this delicious spot.

White River Fish Market & Restaurant, 1708 N. Sheridan Rd., North Tulsa, Tulsa, OK 74115; (918) 835-1910; whiteriverfishmarket .com; Seafood; $$$. The White River Fish Market & Restaurant has been around since 1932 and has fish flown in directly from suppliers on the coastal areas of not only North America but South America as well. Once drawing press like *Gourmet* magazine and the *Splendid Table* radio show to its doors, it still remains a local landmark. It's a family-style restaurant and serves up dishes that are simple, fresh, and above all, flavorful. Choose between (or get both!) the boiled shrimp and oysters on the half shell for starters. Their motto of "you pick em', we'll fix em'" allows you to pick your fresh fish out of the long glass cases that line the dining room. Get your pick fried, broiled, or grilled with a choice of sides like a classic baked potato, pinto beans, or spiced rice. On Tuesday and Wednesday evening, you can feast on lobster tail dinners as well. The atmosphere is casual and you'd be comfortable in just about anything, like your favorite pair of jeans or shorts.

Landmarks

Hank's Hamburgers, 8933 E. Admiral Pl., North Tulsa, Tulsa, OK 74115; (918) 832-1509; hankshamburgers.com; Burgers $$. Hank's Hamburgers has been a staple in Tulsa for over 50 years. Featured in the *New York Times,* on the Food Network, and in the *Tulsa World,* it's still being recommended without reservation! Current owner Dale Jones recently bought this grilled onion burger legend after eating there for 40 years. It was special to him as he and his wife had been dating there most of their married lives. Hank's screams "old-fashioned" with its selection of malts, shakes, fries, and burgers topped with delicious caramelized onions. The other big hit at Hank's is the chocolate-covered peanut butter balls; but be forewarned, they are highly addictive, as is all the diner fare at this Tulsa landmark. Grab a date or a friend and take them over to Hank's.

Nelson's Ranch House, 1547 E. 3rd St., East Tulsa, Tulsa, OK 74120; (918) 584-1337; Southern; $. Nelson's Ranch House has been a Tulsa landmark since 1929. It began as an all-night diner for the gambling crowd, then transitioned into Nelson's Buffeteria, where it was a local favorite among the working crowd for lunch. The name has now changed to Nelson's Ranch House, but the food is still the same and they still offer old-fashioned, home-cooked goodness. Diners can go through an all-you-can-eat buffet and get comfort food staples like chicken-fried steak and cream gravy, mashed potatoes, and fried okra. There are also specials you can order like fried catfish, chicken potpie, or baked spaghetti. And you can't escape without trying one of their truly gigantic pieces of pie like lemon meringue. It'll nicely round out your home-style meal and make you feel like you've just eaten your mama's cooking.

Specialty Stores, Markets & Producers

Pancho Anaya Mexican Bakery, 11685 E. 21st St., East Tulsa, Tulsa, OK 74128; (918) 234-3000; facebook.com/MexicanBakery. If you have a love for Mexican baked goods, you should seek out Pancho Anaya in East Tulsa. Owner Francisco Pancho Anaya is a fourth-generation baker from Mexico. Here you pick up a pair of tongs and a tray and hand-pick your take-home treats like churros, *empanadas de crema, pan dulce, telera, bolillo, donas* and their famous *tres leches* cake. The *tres leches cake* is boxed up in small individual portions and the light cake is soaked as it should be in a sweet three-milk mixture and topped with whipped cream. If you visit this sweet gem, you'll see why most of local Mexican restaurants use Pancho Anaya as a source for freshly baked *torta* bread, and you'll probably want to take some home as well!

Stock Pot, 7223 E. 41st St., East Tulsa, Tulsa OK 74145; (918) 627-1146. Looking for the place where Tulsa chefs buy their equipment? Look no further. The Stock Pot is your go-to place to buy those pots and pans used in professional kitchens as well as other kitchen items and gadgets on every home cook's wish list. You can also buy famous chef-line kitchenware as well as reasonably priced restaurant-grade tools. Choose from their extensive selection of baking sheets, knife sharpeners, whisks, cake domes, tortilla presses, sake bottles, and rolling pins, to name just a few! The Stock Pot also houses a fully stocked cooking school kitchen with top-view projection cameras to show off visiting chefs' cooking skills while the audience watches from raised seating. Cooking classes are held throughout the year, so check the store for classes during your visit.

South Tulsa, Southern Hills & Jenks

This chapter encompasses the southern sections of Tulsa, including Southern Hills, an exclusive country club area. Southern Hills is also home to Oral Roberts University, and college areas are usually known for housing many wonderful coffee shops, cafes, bistros, and ethnic restaurants. Jenks brings entertainment by way of the Oklahoma Aquarium, the Riverwalk Crossing, and is known for its antiques shopping. This area has small-town charm and is developing constantly, boasting riverfront eateries like the Riverwalk Crossing, a fun shopping and eating shoreline experience.

Asian Cuisine, 4710 E. 51st St., South Tulsa, Tulsa, OK 74135; (918) 610-8883; Chinese; $. Where do foodies go to get genuine Cantonese food in Tulsa? They head to Asian Cuisine. There you will find roast duck in Chinese spices and you can order delectable items like clay pots and salt and pepper calamari, strongly flavored with jalapeño. Make sure you ask for the Cantonese menu and not the American one because the authentic offerings are why locals come back again and again. Try the clams in the black bean sauce as they are fresh and rich and deliciously exotic. If you favor duck, call ahead and ask them to make you their Peking duck, which lacks the grease of the regular roasted duck and it is outstanding. If you feel like splurging, the lobster in ginger scallion sauce is fantastic. Take a break from that Americanized Chinese food you're used to and try something genuine in Asian cuisine. You'll be so glad you gave it a try.

Bodean Seafood, 3376 E. 51st St., South Tulsa, Tulsa, OK 74135; (918) 749-1407; bodean.net; Seafood; $$$$. Mention the word "seafood" in Tulsa and you're likely to be pointed to this classic seafood restaurant and market that's been pleasing the locals since 1968. Voted by Tulsans as "Best Seafood Restaurant" in the Urban Tulsa ABOT awards for several years running, Bodean's has the benefit of serving up the fresh food flown in twice daily and delivered into their market in their adjoining restaurant and lounge. Sit in the lounge and enjoy oysters on the half shell for a mere $1.50 each, or dine formally and enjoy them in a variety by ordering the Oysters Four Ways. On Sunday and Monday, they offer a chef's tasting menu featuring three wines matched with a 3-course meal and on weekends there is live entertainment. For dinner, enjoy their challah bread while waiting on a delicious offering of seared scallops topped with apple chutney and swimming in red curry coconut sauce. And don't forget to visit the market on your way out!

Charlie Mitchell's Modern Pub, 4848 S. Yale Ave., South Tulsa, Tulsa, OK 74135; (918) 728-8181; charliemitchells.com; Pub Food; $$. Although he once played professionally for the North American Soccer League for the Tulsa Roughnecks (and later coached them) and the New York Cosmos, Charlie Mitchell has awakened another love in Tulsa: Scottish food. After opening a chain of Charlie Mitchell's, he got out of the restaurant business in 1995 and recently ventured back with this eatery. Here you can find European dishes like fish-and-chips and shepherd's pie but also new, updated favorites named after his favorite players, like the Rochester Lancer Dip, a flavorful blend of spinach and artichoke. The Forfar Bridie's Shepherd's Pie at Charlie Mitchell's is topped with a puff-pastry crust instead of potatoes, which is in character with the Scottish version and is a fun change. Also on the menu are fantastic ribs, burgers, and the like, as well as an all-you-can-eat Sunday buffet of breakfast fare and other dishes.

Duke's Southern Kitchen, 10441 S. Regal Blvd., South Tulsa, Tulsa, OK 74133; (918) 364-3853; dukestulsa.com; Southern; $$. Tim Baker dreamed up Duke's Southern Kitchen under the inspiration of John Wayne. That's right, folks, and this eatery, which sports memorabilia of the Duke himself on the walls and is located in the SpiritBank Event Center in Bixby, sports fun as well with some great Southern comfort food for the rest of us to enjoy. The flavors are taken from Tim's memories of his travels in his younger years. From the drink menu offerings of Lynchburg lemonade, Sazeracs, and mint juleps, to their nice wine list, to their appetizer menu of delicious crispy fried green tomatoes and shrimp and grits, you'll feel like you've traveled to Louisiana and Georgia all in the comfort of Duke's cozy dining room.

French Hen Bistro & Wine Bar, 7143 S. Yale Ave., South Tulsa, Tulsa, OK 74136; (918) 492-2596; frenchhentulsa.net; French; $$$$. This little hidden treasure in Southern Hills has pleased romantics for 30 years. When the restaurant went up for sale a few years back, current owner Kathy Bondy couldn't resist purchasing the fine-dining establishment and making it her own. The restaurant is tucked away in the middle of the Lighthouse Shopping Center, and Kathy consulted with legendary chef Kurt Fleischfresser from Oklahoma City to build the new menu, which also keeps some of the old favorites as well. The patio is charming and the decor inside is pleasant and warm. Begin your dining experience with the forest mushroom tart and its tangy chèvre, and for dinner try the grilled duck breast nestled in a brandy peppercorn cream (or you can opt to have it with orange and cherry glace). French Hen also doubles as a great lunch spot, where you can order the beef bourguignon *en croûte* capped off with crispy fried onions or go a bit more casual with a truffled egg salad sandwich. Their impressive wine list makes them one of the preferred places to take that special date when dining in the southern end of Tulsa.

India Palace, 6963 S. Lewis Ave., South Tulsa, Tulsa, OK 74136; (918) 492-8040; theindiapalacetulsa.com; Indian; $$. Nestled in a strip mall in Southern Hills, India Palace is considered by many to be the best place for Indian food in Tulsa. Whether you choose to visit their large buffet with menu items like pillau rice, chicken tikka masala, biryani, or naan, or to order something a little more adventurous off the menu like the appetizer of vegetable *ghaji,* a fritter-type patty made of chickpeas, onions, and Indian spices. The Mulligatawny Muglai soup is always good for a starter and is a richly spiced lentil soup with rice and chicken. But the main star of the show here, in my opinion, is the tandoori chicken and prawns. Get just one taste of either of these dishes, and you'll want to return to the Palace time and time again. Their extensive wine list features wine from California, Australia, Italy, and Chile among other countries and to cool down your palate, I adore the mango pudding with its creamy sweetness.

Michael V's Restaurant & Bar, 8222 E. 103rd St., South Tulsa, Tulsa, OK 74133; (918) 369-0310; michaelvsrestaurant.com; Seafood/Steak House; $$$$. Chef and owner Michael Minden has a culinary pedigree worthy of mention. As a graduate of the Culinary Institute of America, he also was a chef for Walt Disney World and Marriott hotels. Michael's wife and co-owner Carol is the perfect partner in the eatery, having logged some extensive food service miles herself by being director of catering for several big-name hotel chains. Together, the two turn out some of the most memorable fine dining cuisine in Tulsa. Begin your meal with some baked brie that's been apricot glazed, sprinkled with sliced almonds, and baked to perfection and served with fruit and flatbread. Move on to a perfect entree in the veal cordon Bleu, a fun twist of veal slices that are fork-tender and topped with prosciutto, blue cheese, and fresh spinach. Michael V's also offers a lighter side menu to help you achieve that healthy goal you might be reaching for, but you won't miss out on taste with menu items like a Thai peanut salad with shrimp. Whatever the case, your dining experience will be wonderful.

The Ripe Tomato, 8281 S. Harvard Ave., South Tulsa, Tulsa, OK 74137; Southern Hills District, Tulsa, OK 74137; (918) 495-3999; Sandwiches; $. If you want to shop at a truly neat place and then have a great lunch, this is the place to go. Located in the back corner (southeast) of The Market, a store full of individual crafters and home goods housed in private booths, The Ripe Tomato is a one-room bistro that serves up home-made goodness from house-made salad dressings to gourmet sand-wiches to delectable desserts. You'll forget you're inside a store as you feast on salads like the Freaky Greeky, a tasty combination of Parmesan-crusted chicken, feta, black olives, and Roma tomatoes. Chef and owner Lisa Saylor, who has a background in both culinary arts and interior design, names menu items after her children, like the Hannah Banana, a sandwich with sliced bananas, peanut butter, and honey. The soups, like the ever-popular chicken tortilla soup, are wonderful as well. Being a lemon lover myself, for dessert I love the lemon cake with its tart and sweet layers. Vegetarian options are also offered here.

Riverside Grill, 9912 Riverside Pkwy., South Tulsa, Tulsa, OK 74137; (918) 394-2433; riversidegrilltulsa.com; Steak House/ Seafood; $$$$. Once upon a time, Michael Fusco, one of Tulsa's greatest renowned chefs, was working at one of Tulsa's most popular seafood establishments. Soon he took his talent to his own place and designed what eventually became Riverside Grill on the banks of the Arkansas River in Jenks. The current chef, John Foster Oje, being the child of a Hawaiian-Chinese mother and a pastry chef father, takes the flavors of his youth and mixes them with a new twist by offering up a menu worth sampling. His ever-changing menu focuses on fresh and seasonal foods. Here you'll have a choice between tasty offerings like seared Georges Bank U-10 diver scal-lops with wild mushroom ravioli and lemon velouté, and roast prime rib French dip with white cheddar cheese and steak fries. How do you choose? Be assured that no matter your choice, the flavor will be outstanding.

Siegi's Sausage Factory, 8104 S. Sheridan Rd., South Tulsa, Tulsa, OK 74133; (918) 492-8988; siegis.com; Austrian; $$. In 1985, Siegi Sumaruk opened the doors of this Austrian restaurant, which has strong family roots. After working as a butcher and making sausage in Dallas for many years, he began to bring Tulsa the finest sausages he could make. All 20 varieties he makes in his own processing plant are ready to be ordered and sent to you at any time, or you can buy them at the meat market on the property. Sumaruk is now passing the tradition on to his sons and grandsons. If you dine at Seigi's, you can choose from a variety of sausages off the dinner menu, or go a different culinary way and order the other Central European dishes like Hungarian goulash or beef *Rouladen,* an amazing concoction of fork-tender beef, bacon, pickles, and sautéed onions and carrots smothered in a rich brown gravy.

Tres Amigos Mexican Grill & Cantina, 8144 S. Lewis Ave., South Tulsa, Tulsa, OK 74137; (918) 518-5554; tresamigostulsa .com; Mexican; $$. Mexican eateries are a dime a dozen in Oklahoma, so to find one that truly stands out is something worth writing about. Tres Amigos is beautiful inside and so is their food. They don't turn out a slop of bland enchiladas and sauces here. Tres Amigos instead offers up wonderful cuisine like a Mexican Caesar salad embellished with fajita meat and topped with a dressing with a Mexican twist. For dinner, try the Mexican Volcano Rock dish;

I recommend splitting it with a friend or two as it offers five grilled meats, with cheese, avocado, fresh cactus, rice, and *charro* beans. The Cantina also pours some crazy drinks, like a 72-ounce margarita called the Mega Margarita, but there are plenty of other offerings to drink as well.

Waterfront Grill, 120 Aquarium Dr., Jenks, OK 74037; (918) 518-6300; waterfrontgrilljenks.com; Steak House/Sushi; $$$. On the banks of the Arkansas River right next to the Oklahoma Aquarium sits the Waterfront Grill. The restaurant itself is enormous, and if you're looking for patio dining, this is the place to be, though the menu diverges a bit from the main menu. The bar at Waterfront Grill is a favorite after-work stop for full bar fare and offers some lovely cocktails, so sip on one while you sample the cheese toast, as it's addictive in itself. The main highlight of Waterfront's menu is their sushi. They offer everything here from standard rolls to bento boxes and boats and some truly innovative options like the sushi towers in several varieties. Not in a sushi mood? No problem with dishes like the pecan-encrusted trout. Beef lovers will be pleased to know that the Waterfront's steaks are very tender and very delicious.

White Lion Pub, 6927 S. Canton Ave., Southern Hills District, Tulsa, OK 74136; (918) 491-6533; Pub Food; $$. Tucked away on a street in southern Tulsa, you'll find something excitingly unique in White Lion Pub. It's one of the few places in the area that will transport you straight across the ocean to England. Nestled in a smattering of trees, this Tudor-style house has dark wood, dim lighting, and a warm and welcoming pub feel. Start out with the baked brie and all its gooey warm wonderfulness. With menu items not normally seen around these parts, you'll be able to try things like steak and kidney pie, Cornish pasties, or any variety of meat pies. Don't skip out on the mushy peas either—folks rave about them. You can also get the classic fish-and-chips or even a beef Wellington. The White Lion of course has a nice selection of English ale and other beers to complement your meal. The entrance is a bit tricky so look for the Union Jack!

Landmarks

Cardigan's Restaurant & Bar, 6000 S. Lewis Ave., Southern Hills District, Tulsa, OK 74105; (918) 749-9070; Seafood/Steak House; $$. Everything at Cardigan's is made from scratch. Their original location opened nearly 20 years ago, and has remained a favorite among Tulsans ever since. The ambience is nice, with brick walls and flickering sconces, and you'll be greeted with some of their fresh, warm homemade bread for starters. The menu is a diverse offering of everything from nachos to salmon to stir fry, so there is something for everyone at Cardigan's, which makes it a popular family hangout. The French onion soup is absolute heaven for a starter, and the mixed grill is wonderful and a steal coming in at under 20 dollars and offering chicken, steak, and shrimp. Cardigan's has a nice selection of reasonably priced wine by the glass or bottle, which is a welcome treat. There is a second location at 10912 S. Memorial Dr., Tulsa, OK 74133; (918) 394-2273.

Specialty Stores, Markets & Producers

Hebert's Specialty Meats, 2101 E. 71st St., Southern Hills District, Tulsa, OK 74136; (918) 298-8400; hebertsmeats.com. Hebert's is known widely in Tulsa and many parts of the country for their turducken and alligator dips. But that's not all you can order at this Cajun meat market and eatery in Southern Hills. Items available for purchase include stuffed chicken filled with a choice of 12 different stuffings, and a variety of delicious gumbos like shrimp, crab, and crawfish available by the quart. Perhaps you'd like to walk on the wild side and try the alligator wings or the stuffed rabbit? You can do that also. But drop in for lunch or dinner during the week and try some of this Cajun cuisine or better yet, stop in on a Saturday morning between 10 and 11 a.m. and nibble on some beignets and café au lait to get your weekend started off just right.

Spiceology, The Farm Shopping Center, 6524 East 51st Place, South Tulsa, Tulsa, OK 74145; (918) 895-7838; spiceology.net. Peter Gettys, a former electrical engineer, and his wife, Amanda, a former banker, loved gourmet food but had no formal chef training. Their solution? Open this little slice of foodie heaven along with Peter's parents Jesse and Marcy Gettys. The store features over 100 types of spices, herbs, and blends from all around the globe and is your place to go for those hard-to-find items you don't see in typical grocery stores. Try some lemon peel or Belgian cocoa or how about some Indonesian cloves? You might even try some of their custom blends they create themselves, and you can smell and sample them on site before you buy. They also carry the coveted Nielsen-Massey brand of extracts, vanilla-bean paste, and even Himalayan pink salt and a variety of peppercorns, including the *bhut jolokia* pepper (crushed), one of the hottest registering peppers around!

Oklahoma Suburbs

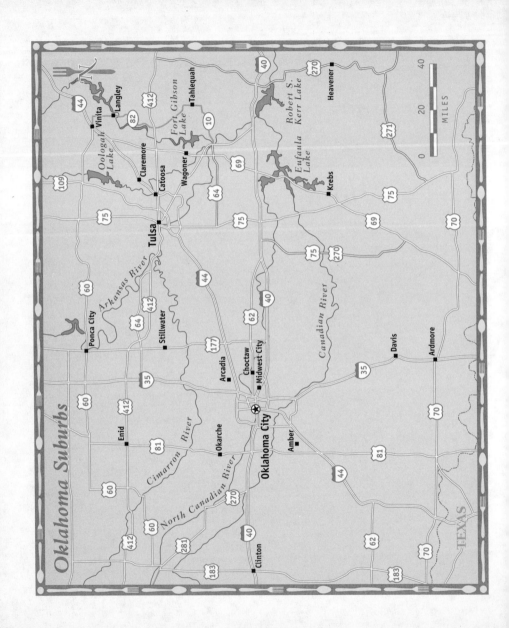

Oklahoma Suburbs

Langley
Vinita
Claremore
Catoosa
Tulsa
Ponca City
Stillwater
Arcadia
Okarche
Enid
Clinton
Oklahoma City
Choctaw
Midwest City
Amber
Tahlequah
Fort Gibson Lake
Oologah Lake
Wagoner
Robert S. Kerr Lake
Eufaula Lake
Heavener
Krebs
Davis
Ardmore
Arkansas River
Cimarron River
North Canadian River
Canadian River

TEXAS

MILES
0   20   40

Oklahoma Suburbs

Outside of Oklahoma City and Tulsa, there are plenty of great places to visit that might be a little less well-known to city folk. These are places that are worth a bit of a drive, and they might be in a small town or in the country. These delectable eateries range from the most beloved fried chicken joint in the state to a family-owned organic resort to the official restaurant of my personal favorite barbecue sauce makers. If you're near or in one of these towns, you'll enjoy visiting these restaurants for a delicious meal. Even if you're on the other side of the state, these places are worth trekking off to with some ambitious foodie friends for a unique weekend visit and a fantastic meal.

Foodie Faves

The Artichoke Restaurant & Bar, 2610 N. 3rd St., Langley, OK 74350; (918) 782-9855; theartichokeatgrand.com; Steak House/Seafood; $$$$. When they saw the 100-year-old farmhouse only a few minutes from the shores of Grand Lake, Artichoke owners Jim and Diane Sellers knew they were going to sell their house and catering business in Oklahoma City, move their boat to the lake, and start a restaurant in that very farmhouse. Chef Mike Allen serves an upscale menu and the visiting vacationers as well as the local set love this eatery so much that you'll have to make a reservation on weekends to even get your foot in the door. The steak soup is a favorite menu item, as is, of course, the artichoke and spinach dip served with pita points. The restaurant sources much of its produce from its own garden right next to the parking lot, which makes everything wonderfully fresh and tasty. The entree menu is classic steak and seafood fare, with shrimp offered three ways. One room in the house is solely devoted to the restaurant bar, which has become a bit of a local hangout where you can grab a cool drink and chat with friends.

The Canebrake Restaurant & Resort, 33241 E. 732nd Rd., Wagoner, OK 74467; (918) 485-1810; thecanebrake.com; Farm to Table; $$$$. This secluded treasure of a resort is the dream of the Bracken family, who moved from the big city and eventually made the resort their home. Named after a bamboo known for purifying and filtering water, this is their intention with their resort: to clear and clean out your body and mind. This kind of healthy thinking follows through in the food they serve at the restaurant. Chef Sam Bracken has a wonderful menu of wholesome dishes packed with flavors from around the world. He uses locally sourced produce and

Home-Grown Chains: Jimmy's Egg

For over 30 years, Jimmy's Egg (jimmysegg.com) has been many Oklahomans' favorite breakfast spot, and with good reason—it has been voted Best Breakfast Place by both the The Oklahoma Reader's Choice Awards and the *Oklahoma Gazette* for the past 15 years. Loc Le was a railroad inspector before he decided to take his life in the breakfast direction, and now it has grown to be a franchise operation in four states with over 30 restaurants. They offer traditional breakfast items on the menu like bacon, ham, steak and eggs, or corned beef hash, but my husband and I love their healthy menu items like their sweet potato pancakes and their spinach and mushroom egg-white omelet. Jimmy's has expanded their menu to offer lunch as well, with really good burgers and sandwiches and smaller lunch portions of pot roast and chicken quesadillas. The kids' menu at this place makes it a family favorite so head over to Jimmy's Egg and try them out.

fresh sustainable seafood, free-range meats, and whole grains. The menu revolves around what's seasonal and the kitchen is frequently open for cooking classes and wine dinners. You'll find main courses like smoked chicken, ancho-rubbed with lime-cilantro yogurt sauce, and salads like the vegetable ribbon salad with miso dressing. You can't help but leave this place feeling good about yourself in a delicious way.

The Cellar at Main Street Wine Depot, 117 E. Main St., Ardmore, OK 73401; (580) 223-4441; Wine Bar; $$. Located in old Ardmore in a building that's been around for over 100 years, Jadean Fackrell and her husband Ken turn out some delicious fare at The Cellar. In the upstairs portion of the Depot, the couple opened a wine store in 2007 with not only wine accessories and gifts, but kits to make your own wine. They also give free winemaking classes every two to three weeks. Located in the original underground tunnels of Ardmore below the wine store is the restaurant, which opened in 2009 with the couple's daughter-in-law Chef Kelly Jo at the helm. Try the Black and Blue Panzanella Salad with shavings of Black Angus steak, sun-dried tomatoes, and asparagus. On Sunday, they have a marvelous brunch featuring items like a smoked salmon frittata or chicken and waffles. They are open for lunch Mon through Thurs and lunch and dinner Fri and Sat.

Eischen's Bar, 109 N. 2nd St., Okarche, OK 73762; (405) 263-9939; Pub Food; $$. When I first moved to Oklahoma City, I quickly heard about the legend of Eischen's chicken. About a half-hour drive outside the city, in the small town of Okarche, is Eischen's, a no-frills bar with sawdust on the floor that serves up some of the best fried chicken you'll ever put in your mouth. An entire fried chicken comes out cut apart and breaded in some kind of wonderful light and crispy breading with sliced onions and pickles. Sides are sparse but you can order a paper boat filled with fried okra that will feed an army. There are far more beer choices than there are side dishes at Eischen's, so head out to Okarche, belly up to the bar or grab a table, and get one of the 4,000 whole chickens Eischen's dishes out weekly. See why people drive from all over the place for their delectable chicken.

Hammett House Restaurant, 16161 W. Will Rogers Blvd., Claremore, OK 74017; (918) 341-7333; hammetthouse.com; Southern; $$. What started in the 1960s as a family restaurant by LaNelle Hammett was carried on and re-created in the 1990s by current owners Bill and Linda Biard. Pastry chef Patsy VanDeventer still uses LaNelle's original recipes to bake their famous pies as well as the delicious mashed potato rolls served alongside the entrees. Everything is homemade at the Hammett House including the soups. Try a hand-tenderized, hand-battered country-fried steak made just like your grandma would make if you lived in the South. In fact, that's exactly what the food is like at The Hammett House—Southern comfort food at its finest. And seriously, don't leave without having a slice of one of those pies. I'd recommend the Sizzlin' Apple

Delight—it comes in a sizzling iron skillet with hot brandy-butter sauce and ice cream. Hammett House is closed Mon.

Head Country BBQ Restaurant, 1217 E. Prospect, Ponca City, OK 74601; (580) 767-8304; headcountry.com; Barbecue; $$. What began in 1945 as a home barbecue sauce recipe from Donovan Fred Head later escalated into a huge business selling sauce and spices to several states plus a full-blown restaurant. This is the go-to sauce my kids love at home, and if we're out of it, they're grumpy. You can visit the restaurant in the company's hometown of Ponca City, but you'll be faced with some choices. How would you like the dilemma of picking from one of six sandwich offerings at this smoky and sweet eatery? And those are just the sandwiches. There are also turkey, hot links, ribs, brisket, and a bunch of side dishes ranging from deviled eggs to BBQ baked potatoes. Once you visit Head Country and sample their famous sauce, you're going to have a longing for it as we do.

Ken's Steaks & Ribs, 406 E. Main St., Amber, OK 73004; (405) 222-0786; facebook.com/KensSteaksAndRibs; Barbecue/Steak House; $$$. Head 10 minutes north of Chickasha, and you'll arrive at a building that is part gas station, part steak house. But don't let that deter you! There is no menu at Ken's, but your server will give you the lowdown on what they have and while you wait they'll bring you out one of the smoky and wonderful barbecue ribs to tide you over. The offerings are chicken, ribs, steak, and prime rib, and the beef is all locally sourced from Pennar Ranch and are grass-fed

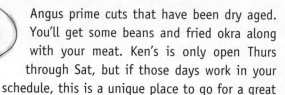

Angus prime cuts that have been dry aged. You'll get some beans and fried okra along with your meat. Ken's is only open Thurs through Sat, but if those days work in your schedule, this is a unique place to go for a great steak. If you're visiting the restaurant during the Christmas season, make it a point to head to Chickasha for their wonderful display of Christmas lights.

Molly's Landing, 3700 N. Hwy. 66, Catoosa, OK 74015; (918) 266-7853; mollyslanding.com; Steak House/Seafood; $$$$. Located on Historic Route 66, Molly's Landing has been here since 1984. Linda Powell had a log cabin added to the property and then began decorating it with charm. Now this part gift shop, part eatery is an Oklahoma legend where she sells her handmade jewelry and her sons help run the restaurant. The restaurant sits on the bank of the Verdigris River and they serve up a menu of steaks, quail, chicken, and seafood. They also offer up Hawaiian pit-style chicken (made by request for parties) from their pit outside. Try the prawns and rice made with special seasoning or the spicy grilled quail for a different flavor. Pick a wine from the extensive wine list to pair with whatever you choose. Fancy a big game of chess? As an added bonus, Molly's Landing boasts a human-size chessboard outside for your enjoyment.

Old Germany, 15920 SE 29th St., Choctaw, OK 73020; (405) 390-8647; oldgermany.com; German; $$$. In 1976 the Turek family, with little left in their pockets, opened a small restaurant with a limited menu in Choctaw. Worried that diners might not be open-minded at first about authentic German cuisine, they slowly introduced the food onto their menu until it became what it is today. True to its name, Old Germany offers up classic old-world recipes and a huge selection of German beer. Mike Turek manages the restaurant while his sister Chef Jutta Wolff helms the kitchen. Together they have a winning restaurant that people drive across the state just to get to. To get your taste buds working, start off with their *cevapcici* appetizer of eight homemade beef sausages—don't worry, they're small enough that you won't spoil your appetite for one of their veal schnitzels smothered in an amazing mushroom sauce. Accompanying their selection of German meats are other delicious offerings like tangy German potato salad and spaetzle. Their drink selection is endless with a bevy of German staples like Rumple Minze, brandies, bourbons, and scotches, and they have quite the selection of German draught beers as well in various sizes.

Panevino Wine & Tapas Bar, 123 W. Randolph, Enid, OK 73701; (580) 237-8488; panevinowinebar.com; Wine Bar; $$. Panevino originally wasn't intended to be a wine bar, but a wine store. The owners intended to sell wonderful wines and accessories, but due to Oklahoma law, the accessory part just wasn't going to work out. Thus the wine bar and restaurant were created, and thank goodness it was! Nevermind that the steaks are hand cut and the menu is ever changing depending on what's fresh—tapas is the star here. You can order new twists on tapas like blue cheese fondue or a roasted garlic head with a baguette or even smoked Scottish salmon to go with one of the great wines off the extensive wine list. If you want to get away from the big city or happen to be driving near Enid, be sure to stop in.

POPS, 660 W. Hwy. 66, Arcadia, OK 73007; (405) 928-7677; route66.com; Burgers; $. Drive northeast of Oklahoma City and you'll see a giant 66-foot spiraled pop bottle begin to appear along the horizon. A sleek, modern gas station is located right at the base of the bottle, and it's also one of the most visited state landmarks around. The food on offer at the diner inside is a big reason why POPS sees so many visitors year in and year out. The diner boasts almost 600 ice-cold sodas from all over the world including over 65 varieties of root beer alone. Inside you can sit alongside a giant glass wall composed of all kinds of colorful soda bottles and munch on American classics like hamburgers, chicken-fried steak, sandwiches, and salads, along with your carbonated beverage of choice. POPS also serves up some mean shakes at their Shake Shop, where you can have a float made with or without pop! The Pops Ripper Dog is a favorite, with an all-beef hot dog deep fried and topped with sauerkraut, mustard chow-chow, cheddar, and tomatoes on a poppy-seed bun. They also have great desserts, including root beer bread pudding and a make-your-own ice cream sandwich sundae. POPS is a must-visit for families.

The Rancher's Club, H103 Student Union, Stillwater, OK 74078; (405) 744-2333; Steak House; $$$$. The Rancher's Club is a cowboy-cultured place with white tablecloths, cowhide rugs, and antler chandeliers. But this isn't some honky-tonk dive. The leather seating, roaring fireplace, and their fine wine list make The Rancher's Club elegant, yet casual. And the food? You come here for the steaks, which are hand selected, hand cut, USDA Prime Beef. These cuts are some of the best you'll have anywhere in the state and are truly a melt-in-your-mouth experience. The eatery is staffed with students from Oklahoma State's top-rated hotel and restaurant school. They also offer Berkshire pork chops, Peking duck, and petite free-range chicken along with lobster and daily fresh fish. Those dishes are all well and good, but most people continue to rave about the steaks after their experience at The Rancher's Club.

Rusty Barrell Supper Club, 2005 N. 14th St., Ponca City, OK 74601; (580) 765-6689; rustybarrell.biz; Steak House; $$$. This mysterious little supper club is a tad hard to locate at the back of a strip mall and has a unique entrance. Once you find the orange door, you have to ring the bell to get in. Grab a chilled pewter plate and dish up your own salad off their fresh and crisp salad bar. And then watch the line cooks grill over an open-air grill in the dining room where the smell wafts throughout the entire eatery to make your mouth water. People have stopped here from every state in the United States and return time and time again for their great steaks. They also offer other grilled meats like chicken, seafood, pork chops, and prime rib. Their signature sauce may just be what makes the steak. They also have a charming lounge upstairs where you can grab a drink and gaze over the railing to see the workings of the grill below.

Sam & Ella's Chicken Palace, 419 N. Muskogee Ave., Tahlequah, OK 74464; (918) 456-1411; Pizza; $$. If you're looking for fried chicken at Sam & Ella's, you might have been misled. Chicken is actually only on the menu twice, but not in the form you might expect, for you see Sam & Ella's is a pizza place. The name comes from the decor, which features the feathered barnyard animal, and the pizza is touted statewide as one of the best. The garlic cheese bread with marinara sauce is delicious, as are their baked mushroom caps stuffed with artichoke spinach dip. Perhaps the hottest menu item going is the Rock Island Red pizza with marinara, honey-drizzled ham, mushrooms, sweet onions, and pineapple. If you prefer a salad, the large is enough for two and they also offers sub "samwiches," which is where you'll find that chicken.

Seoul Garden, 6012 SE 15th St., Midwest City, OK, 73110; (405) 732-3055; Korean; $. Sometimes the simple things in life are the most delicious. Such is the case at Seoul Garden. This Korean-style diner usually only has two employees working at one time, Mr. and Mrs. Kim, he in the back cooking and she maintaining the storefront and waiting tables. The Korean food at Seoul Garden is authentically fantastic with offerings of traditional dishes like *dot* *sol bibimbap, bulgogi* (Korean barbecue) and *jap chae,* three of my personal favorites. Mrs. Kim will bring you out an entire table of kimchee while you wait and you can also pick an Asian-style drink out of the glass counter up front or opt for the hot barley tea and complimentary miso soup out of the large thermos dispensers on the counter. Complimentary with each dish is a fresh, crispy spring roll and pork tempura-battered bites. Find out why we often make the drive out to Midwest City to fulfill our craving for Seoul Garden.

Smokin' Joe's Rib Ranch, 1793 Hwy. 77 S., Davis, OK 73030; (580) 369-2818; smokinjoesribranch.com; Barbecue; $$. Smokin' Joe's is the cause for a regular pilgrimage to Davis, Oklahoma, because people become addicted to their delicious barbecued meats and fixings. Joe Wells originally opened up a small place as a hobby to smoke ribs a couple of days a week and it has now evolved into a full-time family business that folks come to time and time again. The ribs and brisket are marinated each night and then smoked all day until they are tender, smoky, and absolutely fall-off-the-bone wonderful. If you haven't tried smoked bologna, Oklahoma style, you're going to be in heaven at Joe's. The portions are generous and as an added bonus Smokin' Joes is part restaurant, part RV park. Munch on some delectable barbecue and spend the night with an amazing view of the Arbuckle Mountains.

Southern Belle Restaurant, Hwy. 59 N., Heavener, OK 74937; (918) 653-4458; facebook.com/southernbelleheavener; Southern; $. Families and visitors love to dine inside this old, restored train car (which once carried World War II troops) while eating some delicious home-cooked comfort food. Owner Debbie Crabtree's brother, while driving a school bus for a living, found the old railcar and had a dream to make a restaurant in it. The Southern Belle Chicken is all the talk at Southern Belle Restaurant. The secret marinade makes it juicy and tender, the breading is superb, and the dipping sauce is to die for. Other offerings include Southern staples like fried catfish, club sandwiches, loaded fries, and homemade pies.

Tokyo Pot, 108 W. 10th Ave., Stillwater, OK 74074; (405) 372-8898; Japanese; $$. Do you shabu-shabu? If you don't, you should, and if you're in the Stillwater area or even if you aren't, make your way to this place. The concept of Tokyo Pot's shabu-shabu is that you sit at a table where two burners are sunk into the center. Two different wonderful broths are heated in pots and a variety of paper-thin sliced meats and vegetables are brought to the table, where you fondue them in the broth Japanese style. Dean Chen, part owner and front of house manager, is the life of the party and makes the entire experience a riot with his sake bomb and Sapporo offerings, crazy hats, and his knowledge of making the entire shabu experience something memorable that will have you longing to go back.

White Dog Hill, 22901 N. Route 66, Clinton, OK 73601; (580) 323-6922; Steak House; $$$. Nelson King spent three years restoring the old stone building that once housed Clinton's country club along Historic Route 66 into the restaurant that it is today. The eatery sits atop a hill overlooking the scenic countryside and the town below. He named it after one of his two dogs and went ahead and opened a separate bar at the White Dog—The Beanie Bar—which is named after his other canine. White Dog Hill's menu is unpretentiously classic with giant cheese boards, wine, and wonderful steaks. There are also Cornish game hens, smoked pork chops, and some wonderfully creative salads. At the end of the meal, when the sun is setting, have a glass of wine paired with one of their fantastic desserts like lemon pecan pie and sit on the Adirondack chairs overlooking the twinkling lights of the city. Oh, and did I mention there is a rumored ghost named Dottie who frequents the old stone building? Find out about her story when you visit!

 **Landmarks**

Clanton's Cafe, 319 E. Illinois Ave., Vinita, OK 74301; (918) 256-9053; clantonscafe.com; Southern; $. Generations of diners have been dropping in to dine at Clanton's Cafe since 1927. Located in the northwest corner of the state, it is the oldest family-run operation along Historic Route 66 and is still going strong. Their timeless favorite chicken-fried steak was featured in *Gourmet* magazine and they have also been featured on *Diners, Drive-Ins and Dives*. Here you're going to find classic diner fare such as fried mushrooms and jalapeño poppers on the starter menu as well as one item you may not be familiar with: calf fries (keep an open mind!). They also have dinner items like pot roast stuffed potatoes, delicious burgers, and sandwiches, and a 16 ounce T-bone. But seriously, get the chicken-fried steak. They do it and do it well. See why people traveling Route 66 make it a regular stop when heading this way.

Specialty Stores, Markets & Producers

Lovera's Famous Italian Market, 95 W. 6th St., Krebs, OK 74554; (800) 854-1417. Lovera's is a third-generation family-owned Italian market run by Sam Lovera. What was once his grandparents' grocery store has now been refined into a charming gourmet market that makes some of the best Italian homemade sausages, cheeses, and olive oils in the state. You'll see their fare all over Oklahoma in markets and specialty shops alike. From their own line of marinara sauces, spices, rubs, and antipasti, to imported items like Italian coffee beans, olive oils, and tomatoes, you'll find an Italian food lover's dream at Lovera's. It would be a crime to walk away without a sampling of their famous caciocavallo cheese, which you'll see made fresh, hand stretched in the back, and hung up to age a bit. I love the smoked version on crackers with sun-dried tomatoes in oil. Delicious! Lovera's also makes their own famous sausages and pasta, which you can take home as well.

Oklahoma Breweries

The world of craft beer is expanding in the United States like crazy. Over the past 5 or so years, Oklahoma's local beer selection has been truly growing by leaps and bounds and our state can proudly boast several solid local craft breweries producing some top-shelf product.

Battered Boar Brewery, 14801 Metro Plaza Blvd., Edmond, OK, 73013, batteredboar.com. Battered Boar prides itself on being a small-batch brewery. Using all natural ingredients, Battered Boar's beers are bottle conditioned, or individually bottled and left for natural carbonation and development. This condition is called "priming" and sometimes referred to as "living beer," and the natural action of the yeast (as opposed to filtered beer under high pressure gas injection) is used to ferment their beers. Battered Boar is a relatively young brewery, open since 2009 and founded by Edmond, Oklahoma's Mike Sandefur. The brewery began with a few solid offerings, namely Company Man Pale Ale and Briar Patch Amber. Recently my husband and I attended a taste testing of Oklahoma brewed beer, and we were both fans of Battered Boar's Chucks Pumpkin Ale (made with Oklahoma sugar pumpkins) and also their Coconut Cream Stout, two of their newest creations.

Choc Beer Company, 120 SW 8th St., Krebs, OK 74554; (918) 423-2042. The year was 1903, and 11-year-old Pete Piegari arrived in Krebs, Oklahoma, with his parents from San Gregorio Mango, Italy. At the age of 21, he was involved in a coal mining accident and injured his leg badly enough that he was unable to work in the mines. But he didn't let that keep him down, and hatched the idea to brew a beer to sell to the miners during their breaks using an old Indian Territory recipe. Changing his name to Pete Prichard, this home brewer founded and began selling Choc beer from his home and later opened Pete's Place restaurant, which became (and still is) a hit with the Italian community of Krebs. While Prohibition tried to shut down his production of beer, in the 1990s Pete's grandson Joe reintroduced Choc beer as a legal brew for Pete's Place customers, and Choc Beer became a favorite among Oklahomans. Under the careful watch of Brewmaster Michael Lalli, a Pete's Place employee since the age of 16, Choc now produces 12 craft brews, each very different from the others, ranging from their Belgian-style White to their one of a kind Saison. From the mill house to the mash tun to the brew kettle to the tanks, Choc is one beer company to keep watching. In 2009, Choc won the gold medal for their Belgian-style Dubbel at the 2009 Great American Beer Festival. Expect to see more great things coming from this little Italian community of Oklahoma in the future.

COOP Ale Works, 1124 NW 51st St., Oklahoma City, OK 73118; (405) 842-2667; coopaleworks.com. COOP Ale Works began as any great beer does, with a few home brews that became pretty popular among friends. After that, Mark Seibold, J. D. Merryweather, and Daniel Mercer took their show on the road for a couple of years, learning as much as they could from breweries around the United States, Central America, and Europe. Returning to Oklahoma City, the trio founded COOP in 2008, along with Head Brewer Blake Jarolim, and the brewery has become a local favorite ever since. They have six original beers that are available seasonally and year round, including some fun offerings like their wildly popular Oktoberfest, a strong German malt with hops from Central Bavaria. Their Horny Toad Cerveza is crisp and clean, the Gran Sport Porter is chocolaty and robust, and the DNR Belgian Style Golden Ale has notes of dried fruit, cinnamon, and vanilla. COOP was recently selected to pour at Savor 2012, one of the biggest craft beer events in the nation. See why local foodies are die-hard COOP fans by trying one of their great brews.

Marshall Brewing Company, 618 S. Wheeling Ave., Tulsa, OK 74104; (918) 292-8781; marshallbrewing.com. Marshall Brewing opened up in 2008 in a large facility outside downtown Tulsa and became the first brewing establishment in the city since World War II. Eric Marshall, the founder Marshall Brewing Company, had the brew business in his blood. His father David, who loved all things Scottish, actually converted a vacant bedroom in the family home into a Scottish pub. Eric himself studied in Germany furthering his love of great brews, apprenticed under some great German brewmasters, and returned to Tulsa after a brewing stint in Pennsylvania. Marshall recently expanded its tank operation because the demand was greater than they could handle. Marshall products can now be found at around 200 bars and eateries around Oklahoma with plans on advancing into other states in the near future. Marshall Brewing Company boasts four year-round favorites, including their India Pale Ale and an Old Pavilion Pilsner, inspired by Eric's time spent in Germany. They also introduce seasonal brews like their Revival Red Ale, named as a tribute to the red dirt of Oklahoma, but don't worry, it tastes much better than its namesake!

Mustang Brewing Company, 502 N. Meridian Ave., Oklahoma City, OK 73107; (405) 943-0100; mustangbrewing.com. Tim and Carmen Schoelen created a business plan, sold their house, cashed in their 401K plans, rented a new house, and began to brew beer in their garage. In the summer of 2009, the couple sold their first pint of Mustang at James E. McNellie's Public House in Oklahoma City. Fast-forward to 2011, when Mustang sold over 24,000 cases of beer in Oklahoma alone! They have expanded their operation to Arkansas as well, and their beer is being served in over 200 eateries and bars. While the beer itself started out being brewed in another state, plans are under way to move the entire production to Oklahoma. The Schoelens wanted to create a craft beer that would pull in the masses, not just the high-end beer lovers, and based on the way their sales are growing, they've done just that. They feature four year-round brews such as the 2011 Word Beer Championship gold medal winner Washita Wheat, made with Oklahoma red wheat. They also have seasonals in four varieties and a special release with their Session '33, which is a whimsical nod to Prohibition repeal. Look for the big M on the bottles and take a sip of one of these great brews.

Redbud Brewing Company, Oklahoma City, OK; redbudbrewing .com. This young brewery opened in 2011 and while perhaps it's one of the youngest breweries around, their brewmaster Chase Healey is anything but a novice when it comes to brewing the good stuff. After being the first brewmaster for COOP Ale Works, Chase left to start his own company, which earned him immediate respect among beer lovers. Redbud currently offers two different beers, the Redbud Pale Ale, their everyday drinking beer with a bright hop flavor and a touch of malt, and a cuvée beer called Cuvée 1, a Belgian-style golden ale with big fruit and spice notes. Chase prides himself on making a craft beer he himself would love and on the immediate release of his pale ale, locals bars clamored to add it to their beer rotation. More brews are in the works at this new gem so stay tuned to see what's coming next.

Recipes

Dock Soup

Ludivine's Chef Jonathon Stranger and Chef Russ Johnson have been innovative in their "New Prairie Cuisine" since day one. Their entire philosophy is to use and cook the local bounty found in Oklahoma, from produce and to dairy. This includes foraging for dock, a wild and leafy herb used in this soup, which Jonathon tells me is his personal favorite. The simple idea that a foraged herb can be made into a delicious soup is but one example of what makes these chefs and Ludivine so special. If you can't find dock, or sorrel at your local farmer's market or grocery store, you may substitute a leafy green like swiss chard.

Makes 4 servings

2 tablespoons lard or olive oil	¾ cup chicken stock
½ cup diced yellow onion	½ teaspoon nutmeg
1 tablespoon finely diced shallot	1 teaspoon orange zest
1 tablespoon chopped garlic	4 cups dock cleaned, packed
¾ cup Riesling	Salt, to taste

Garnish

2 teaspoons crème fraîche	1 teaspoon caviar
1 teaspoon orange zest	

Place a saucepot over medium heat and add the lard. When the lard has melted and starts sizzling, add the onion, shallot, and garlic. When they have become translucent and slightly caramelized, add the Riesling and reduce the liquid by half. Add the chicken stock and reduce the liquid by a third. Add the nutmeg, 1 *teaspoon of the orange zest, and dock into the saucepot and cook for 3 minutes or until all of the dock has wilted. Pour the soup base into a Vitamix or blender, and puree on high until all of the mixture is smooth in texture. Season with salt, to taste.*

Divide the soup among four bowls. Top with the crème fraîche first, then the orange zest, and finish with the caviar on top.

Courtesy of Jonathon Stranger, Chef and Owner of Ludivine (p. 132)

Sesame Vin Dressing

Bruce Rinehart made this recipe when he lived back east in Boston and brought it with him to us lucky folks here in Oklahoma. He uses it in his restaurants over fish or as a salad dressing. This dressing is wonderful over a spinach or Asian salad but he says it's even better over fresh sea bass or halibut! Rococo specializes in many fantastic seafood dishes, each one more delicious than the next.

Makes 12 servings

1 tablespoon ginger, chopped
1 cup rice wine vinegar
2 tablespoon chile garlic paste
⅓ cup white vinegar
½ cup soy sauce
¼ cup oyster sauce

1 tablespoon granulated sugar (fine)
1 teaspoon fish sauce
¼ cup sesame oil
1½ cups grape-seed oil

Marinate ginger in the vinegar for 2 hours.

Add all other ingredients excluding oils and mix well. Whisk oils into the mixture creating an emulsion. This can also be accomplished by mixing all ingredients in a blender.

Courtesy of Bruce Rinehart, Owner of Rococo Restaurant & Fine Wine (p. 44)

Tomato & Herb Tart

Executive Chef Jimmy Stepney of Boulevard Steakhouse started his food career as a cook who prepared the food trays for in-flight meal service. Of course, his airline food was actually good. He was also a member of the opening team at the Astrodome in Houston, where he worked in the sky boxes with players and VIPs. You're going to feel like a VIP as well if you bake up this delicious tart that Jimmy was kind enough to share.

Makes 8 servings

- 1 package phyllo sheets (7 sheets)
- ½ cup butter (2 sticks), melted
- 1½ cups grated Parmesan cheese
- ¾ cup thinly sliced onion
- ½ cup grated mozzarella cheese
- 12–15 Roma tomatoes, seeded and thinly sliced
- ¼ cup fresh thyme, leaves only, chopped
- ½ teaspoon fresh cracked pepper

Preheat oven to 350°F. Using a half sheet pan or a cookie sheet, lay out a single sheet of phyllo and brush with melted butter and sprinkle lightly with Parmesan cheese. Keep repeating until you use all seven sheets. On top of the last sheet, sprinkle the sweet onions and the mozzarella cheese and top with sliced tomatoes overlapping each other. Sprinkle with Parmesan cheese, chopped thyme, and cracked pepper. Place in the oven and bake for 11 minutes or until crust is golden brown.

Courtesy of Executive Chef Jimmy Stepney of Boulevard Steakhouse (p. 58)

Goat Cheese Cake with Prosciutto, Local Honey & Arugula with Lemon Vinaigrette

Chef Alain Buthion's cuisine at his La Baguette Bistro in Oklahoma City mainly stems from his French roots. However, since settling in Oklahoma City, he fuses his food with other flavors as well. No one makes a better classic vinaigrette than the French, and after tasting Alain's once at a chef event, I've longed for his recipe ever since. Alain advises to make sure you use the best possible Dijon mustard you can get, as the quality will make a huge difference in your vinaigrettes and sauces.

Makes 8 servings

- ¾ cup pecans
- ¾ cup toasted garlic bread crumbs
- 2 tablespoons olive oil (for brushing ramekins)
- 4 slices prosciutto (very thin)
- 1 pound goat cheese (fresh log)
- 2 eggs
- ½ cup heavy cream
- 2 teaspoons chopped fresh rosemary
- 1 teaspoon kosher salt
- 1 teaspoon ground white pepper
- 1 cup honey
- 1 bunch fresh arugula

Preheat oven to 325°F. Make the crust by blending pecans and toasted garlic bread in blender. Brush eight ramekins (around 6-ounce capacity each) with olive oil and divide the powdered bread/pecan mix evenly among them, packing the bottoms. Cut each prosciutto slice in half lengthwise and line the inside of each ramekin with a half prosciutto slice so all the edges are tucked in at the bottom. Mix the goat cheese, eggs, cream, and rosemary, salt, and white pepper for 5 minutes with a mixer and evenly divide among the ramekins. Bake in oven for 15–20 minutes then let cool for 10 minutes. Flip over each ramekin and place crust down on a serving plate. Serve warm and top with honey. Finish with a side of baby arugula and the citrus vinaigrette (recipe below).

Optional—top with chopped apples, pears, oranges, and roasted pecans.

Lemon Vinaigrette

½ cup lemon juice

½ cup Dijon mustard

Zest of 4 lemons

3 cups olive oil

½ teaspoon white pepper

1 teaspoon salt

In the order listed, add to a blender and blend together.

Courtesy of Alain Buthion, Chef and Owner of La Baguette Bistro (p. 86)

Cointreau-Cured Scottish Salmon on Johnnycakes

Chef Jonas Favela grew up in Las Vegas, which introduced his palate to gourmet food. Pair that with a couple of grandmothers who knew how to cook a tasty meal and inspired him to pursue a career in the kitchen, and it's no wonder that he now sports the title of executive chef at Ranch Steakhouse, one of Oklahoma City's premier restaurants. Chef Favela's cuisine could best be described as Southwestern comfort food. If you've never had home-cured salmon, you are in for a treat. You'll never go back to buying the packaged store-bought stuff again after trying this chef's recipe.

Makes 6–8 servings

For the salmon

3 cups granulated sugar

3 cups kosher salt

3–5 pound side of salmon (Scottish is best, but buy the best possible quality you can find)

½ cup Cointreau (Grand Marnier could be a good substitute)

1 medium red onion, thinly sliced

To cure the salmon: Mix sugar and salt together and set aside. Leave skin on salmon and make sure all the bones are removed. Use a pan big enough for the salmon to fit lengthwise and that is at least 2 inches deep. Sprinkle the bottom with the salt/sugar blend, using at least 2 cups.

Lay the salmon down on the skin side, pour the Cointreau over the entire salmon, then sprinkle the salmon with 2 cups of the salt/sugar blend. Place the thinly sliced red onion all over the salmon then cover the entire salmon with the remaining 2 cups of the salt/sugar blend.

Cover and place in refrigerator for at least 24–36 hours. A good firmness in the finished product will let you know it is ready; thicker sides of salmon will take longer than thin. Rub away the salt/sugar and red onions and discard. Rinse the salmon under cold water to remove all the salt/sugar, and make sure to rinse the skin side as well. Pat dry with a towel and refrigerate.

For the Johnnycakes

4 cups yellow cornmeal

2 cups all-purpose flour

1¼ cups white sugar

4 tablespoons baking powder

2 tablespoons salt

6 eggs

3 cups whole milk

Combine all ingredients with mixer until smooth (use paddle attachment).

Drop batter on a buttered griddle on medium to medium-high heat, so that the cakes are about 2 inches in diameter. Flip when golden brown. Thinly slice salmon and serve salmon on johnnycakes.

Courtesy of Executive Chef Jonas Favela of Ranch Steakhouse (p. 73)

Grilled Scallops with Watercress Salsa

I first met Executive Chef Daniel Nemec when he was a guest on my TV segment one morning. He was as much at ease in front of the camera as he is whipping up one of his incredible grilled creations at Mickey Mantle's Steakhouse. When my husband and I go to Mickey Mantle's, we know without a doubt that we are going to be pleased with our culinary adventure there. One can understand why this chef, who oversees five kitchens at various restaurants, is in big demand for his cuisine.

Makes 2 servings

1 cup diced grilled pineapple
½ cup diced tomato
¼ cup chopped cilantro
¼ cup chopped poblano
1 each diced jalapeño
½ cup diced onion
¼ cup lime juice

2 bunches watercress
Salt to taste
White pepper to taste
6 large scallops
¼ cup olive oil for brushing
1 tablespoon lemon pepper

Grill pineapple in saucepan over medium-high heat until caramelized, 5-7 minutes. Combine all ingredients except scallops and lemon pepper in a bowl. Let ingredients set while scallops are on the grill. To prepare scallops, brush each side of them with oil and sprinkle with lemon pepper. Place on a very hot grill and cook for 2 minutes on each side. Place salsa mixture in the center of a plate and arrange scallops on the perimeter. Drizzle with left-over juice from salsa mixture.

Courtesy of Executive Chef Daniel Nemec of Mickey
Mantle's Steakhouse (p. 134)

Tongue & Cheek
(Braised Beef Tongue & Veal Cheek)

Because of his diverse culinary background, his prestigious culinary degree, and his love of true New Mexican cuisine, Marc Dunham has a unique flair for recipes involving fantastic chiles and ingredients from the Southwest. Don't let the tongue in this recipe scare you; it is actually one of the tastiest cuts of meat around and anything Marc dishes up is sure to be delicious. Ask for tongue and veal cheek at your local butcher.

Serves 6

The Brine

1 gallon water
½ pound kosher salt
¼ pound brown sugar
½ ounce curing (pink) salt
2 ounces pineapple vinegar
2 tablespoons black
  peppercorns, cracked

1 tablespoon cumin seed,
  toasted, crushed
2 cloves garlic, crushed
1 beef tongue, trimmed of
  unwanted fat or tissue
2 veal cheeks, trimmed of
  unwanted fat or tissue

Place all the ingredients except the beef tongue and veal cheeks into a 2-gallon stockpot and bring to a boil. Remove and cool to room temperature before using.

Place the beef tongue in the brine and refrigerate for 7 days. Make sure the tongue is kept at 35°F–38°F.

Add the cheeks to the tongue for the last 3 days of brining. Make sure the brine is kept at 35°F–38°F.

Remove the cheeks and tongue and vacuum seal them. Return to the refrigerator immediately to keep under 40°F or cook immediately.

Cook the veal cheeks at 180°F (82°C) for 10 hours sous vide, plunge into an ice-water bath immediately afterward, and cool to 40°F within 2 hours and refrigerate until needed.

Cook the beef tongue at 155°F (68°C) for 36 hours sous vide, plunge into an ice water bath immediately afterward, and cool to 40°F within 2 hours and refrigerate until needed.

Remove both 30 minutes before needed and peel the tongue and trim any unwanted fat. Trim the cheeks of any unwanted fat or tissue.

The Cascabel and Tomato Sauce

8 cascabel chiles, stem removed and seeded

1 teaspoon Tellicherry black peppercorns

1 teaspoon cumin seed

1 pound ripe, local tomatoes

½ yellow onion, cut into 2 quarter pieces

2 bulbs wild garlic (can substitute whole garlic with skin)

Cold water as needed

Salt to taste

Lime juice to taste

½ pint local cherry or teardrop tomatoes, quartered

Salt

Preheat a comal or cast-iron skillet on medium-high heat. Toast the cascabel chiles for 30 seconds per side and remove. Toast the peppercorns and cumin seed for 45 seconds to 1 minute and remove. Take care not to burn. If they burn, adjust the heat and start over.

Add 1 pound of tomatoes, yellow onion, and garlic and char each. The garlic will char in about 2 minutes (if using store-bought garlic, keep the skin on while charring). Char the onion and tomatoes on all sides until evenly charred.

Add all of the above ingredients to a blender and begin to blend. Slowly drizzle in enough cold water until the ingredients just begin to liquefy. Continue to add the water until you reach the desired sauce consistency.

Add the sauce to a saucepot and bring to a simmer, and continue to cook for another 30 minutes. Adjust the seasoning with salt and lime juice, and if the sauce becomes too thick, adjust with water. Taste before serving. Hold warm while preparing the hominy and slicing the tongue and cheek.

The Hominy

2 tablespoons olive oil, and more as needed	2 cloves garlic, sliced thin
¼ cup pepitas	2 cups hominy, drained and rinsed
Juice from ½ lime	1 teaspoon Mexican oregano

Preheat a 10-inch sauté pan on medium heat and add the olive oil.

Add the pepitas and lightly brown, stirring occasionally. This should take about 5–7 minutes.

Add the juice from half a lime and continue to cook for another minute.

Add 2 tablespoons olive oil and the garlic and cook for about 3 minutes, stirring frequently, taking care not to burn the garlic but lightly toast it. Reduce the heat to low.

Add the hominy and Mexican oregano and stir to coat everything evenly. Add a little more olive oil if needed to coat the mixture evenly.

To Plate

Place the quartered cherry tomatoes in a small mixing bowl and lightly salt them. Reserve for plating.

The beef and tongue should be slightly chilled or at room temperature. Cut the veal cheek into half-inch cubes and slice the beef tongue into ⅛-inch slices. Place even portions of tongue and cheek into the center of six bowls. Place even portions of the hominy mixture on top of the tongue and cheek, and pour about 6 to 8 ounces of cascabel tomato sauce on top of and around the tongue and cheek. Place even portions of the lightly salted quartered cherry tomatoes on top of the hominy.

Courtesy of Chef Marc Dunham,
Director of the Francis Tuttle School of Culinary Arts (p. 95)

Grilled Catfish
with a Sweet Potato Tamale

The Coach House's Kurt Fleischfresser's accomplishments range from cooking for presidents to writing, producing, and appearing on The Oklahoma Kitchen. *His international experience includes participating in the Essen und Trinken symposium in Munich to traveling to China on behalf of SUSTA, promoting the United States. Chef Kurt is a member of the James Beard Foundation and the Slow Food movement, which is not surprising at all, because if you've tasted any of his creations that use local Oklahoma ingredients, you'll understand why his praises run far and wide. This recipe is a typical example of taking simple, earthy ingredients and transforming them into an amazing taste of Oklahoma.*

Makes 8 servings

For the Tamale

2 cups roasted sweet potato

¾ cup Japanese panko bread crumbs

½ teaspoon cumin

½ teaspoon ground black pepper

½ teaspoon soy sauce

1 tablespoon balsamic vinegar

¼ teaspoon cayenne pepper

1 teaspooon kosher or sea salt

6 ounces grated Oklahoma cheddar (Christian Farms or Watonga)

8 each dried corn husks (soaked in warm water)

Mix the first eight ingredients together with a fork, until thoroughly mixed but not pureed. Fold the grated cheese into the sweet potato mixture. It is not necessary to be gentle; just mix enough to incorporate the cheese. Oil a muffin tin or any heatproof cylindrical containers that will hold about 4 ounces. Lay in a corn husk so that it goes down one side and up the other with the pointed side sticking up out of the mold. Scoop approximately 4 ounces into each mold; this should compress the corn husks against the inside of the molds. Bake at 350°F for about 12 minutes or until completely heated through and ready to serve.

For the Grilled Catfish

8 (4–6 ounce) catfish fillets	Salt and pepper (to taste)
¼ cup chopped parsley	2 tablespoons olive oil

Preheat the grill or skillet (if not grilling). Pat the fillets down with paper towels to remove excess moisture. Put the parsley, salt, and pepper on the catfish then drizzle the oil over the fillets. Making sure your grill is hot, place the fillets on the grill with the smooth side up (this is the side where the skin was). After about 3 minutes, flip the fillets over. After about 3 more minutes, flip the fillets again in such a way that there will be marking across the previous grill marks. Flip the fish one last time and cook until it is slightly opaque in the center. The fillet should have a great crosshatch grill marks on top with the parsley cooked and intensely green. Let the fish rest for just a couple of minutes before serving.

Chile-Peanut Sauce

¼ cup peanut oil	2 tablespoon tomato puree
1 ancho chile	½ cup peanuts, chopped
3 cloves garlic, finely chopped	1 tablespoon brown sugar
1 yellow onion, finely diced (about 2 cups)	1 teaspoon kosher salt
	3 cups chicken stock
1 teaspoon chile powder	4 leaves fresh basil, cilantro, or parsley, chopped
¼ teaspoon cayenne pepper	
1 teaspoon smoked paprika	1 lime, juiced
2 tablespoon peanut butter	

Heat the oil in a 1-gallon pot. When the oil is hot add the chile, garlic, onion, and the dried spices and stir with a wooden spoon until the onions are cooked; this should be very aromatic. Then add the peanut butter and tomato puree and sauté and stir for about 3 minutes. Then add the rest of the ingredients and reduce by half. This sauce can be made in advance and reheated before use.

Serve over catfish and tamales.

Courtesy of Kurt Fleischfresser, Executive Chef and Owner of The Coach House (p. 82)

Vietnamese Crepe

Chef Zahidah's passion for cooking started long before she opened a restaurant. Born in Cambodia and moving to the United States at the age of 5, she comes from a family of seven brothers and sisters, and cooking was an integral part of daily life for her. What started as impromptu dinner parties turned into a full-service Asian fusion restaurant. I had this dish the first time I went to KEO and it left a memorably delicious impression on me. I love that Zahidah has agreed to include this recipe in the guide, as it signifies the Vietnamese influence in Oklahoma's cuisine.

Makes 6 crepes

For the Filling

1½ tablespoon oil

3 ounces shredded breast of duck meat, cut into bite size pieces

Pinch salt and pepper

½ teaspoon minced garlic

6–7 pieces julienned white onion

1 teaspoon oyster sauce

½ teaspoon soy sauce (**Zahidah** recommends Maggi brand)

2 tablespoons coconut milk

½ teaspoon sugar

Cook your duck by heating wok or frying pan, add 1½ tablespoons of oil, and then add duck. Add a pinch of salt and pepper and stir, not allowing it to burn. Add minced garlic and julienned onion. Cook, stirring for about 2 minutes. Add oyster sauce, soy, coconut milk, and sugar. Keep warm.

For the Crepe

12 ounces prepared rice flour
  or crepe mix
1 egg
1 tablespoon salt
3 cups water

1 cup coconut milk
⅓ cup chopped scallions
1 pinch turmeric
¼ cup bean sprouts

Combine all ingredients and whisk until smooth. Heat medium-sized nonstick skillet over medium heat and pour 4 ounces of batter into pan, enough to coat the bottom of the skillet.

Cover and allow to cook. When one side of crepe is browned, turn over and continue cooking (2–3 minutes on each side). Repeat procedure for remaining five crepes.

Off to one side, top crepe with filling, add bean sprouts, and fold crepe over. Cook 2–3 minutes to allow crepe to brown a little. Serve on dinner plate with salad below.

Salad

1 cup water
½ cup sugar
¼ cup white vinegar
¼ cup sambal oelek
½ cup fish sauce

½ cup chopped lettuce
½ cup cucumber
1 tablespoon crushed peanuts
1 tablespoon julienned carrot

Boil water, sugar, vinegar, sambal oelek, and fish sauce to dissolve sugar, about 1 minute. Let cool. To make salad, arrange lettuce and cucumbers on plate. Drizzle with salad dressing, top with peanuts and carrots.

Courtesy of Chef Zahidah Hyman, President of KEO (p. 169)

Matt's Chicken Pesto Pasta

Chef Matt Kelley is all about using fresh and local produce at his restaurant Lucky's, a foodie favorite in Tulsa, and when he's home cooking for his family, he teaches his daughters how to make this dish that's perfect for our hot Oklahoma summers. It's quick, easy and delicious. Matt's dishes rely on simple, fresh ingredients to bring out the flavors of the food. Serve this with a toasted loaf of your favorite artisan bread and a salad on a hot summer evening.

Makes 4 servings

- 1 cup fresh basil leaves, packed
- 2 cloves garlic
- ¼ cup Parmigiano Reggiano cheese, grated
- ¼ cup toasted pine nuts
- (reserve 1 tablespoon cheese and pine nuts for garnish)
- Salt and pepper to taste
- ¼ cup olive oil

- 3 boneless, skinless chicken breasts (or one whole roasted chicken)
- ¼ cup bottled vinaigrette salad dressing
- 1 (9-ounce) package fresh fettuccini pasta
- 1 pint mixed small heirloom tomatoes

Combine basil, garlic, cheese, pine nuts, and salt and pepper in blender or food processor, and process until ground. Slowly add olive oil as motor runs. Process until desired texture is reached.

Marinate chicken breasts for 3 hours in vinaigrette, then grill until cooked through, or buy cooked roasted chicken and pull meat off chicken.

Cook pasta as manufacturer suggests; strain and cool in cold water, then strain until dry.

When pasta is cool and dry, combine with pesto and top with tomatoes, chicken, and reserved cheese and pine nuts.

Courtesy of Chef Matt Kelley and Brooke Kelley, Owners of Lucky's Restaurant (p. 172)

Moroccan Lamb with Tomato Jam

Chef Ryan Parrott has a passion for creating wonderful Southwest cuisine at his restaurant Local in Norman, Oklahoma, but he offers more than just great food. Chef Ryan knows how to build community and it has made him a beloved favorite of locals. His focus is on flavor and not flair and the equation works perfectly for him. His use of spices in this savory dish is sure to please you as much as his local followers.

1 cup coriander seeds	2 tablespoon cayenne pepper
½ cup cardamom pods	1 whole head of garlic
½ cup cumin seed	1 leg of lamb
½ cup cinnamon	1 cup olive oil
½ cup smoked paprika	Zest and juice of 2 lemons
½ cup turmeric	½ cup honey

Toast coriander seeds, cardamom pods and cumin seed in oven on a baking sheet (dry with no oil) at 350°F up to 7 minutes or until you smell their fragrance. Add spices to spice grinder or mortar and pestle in batches and grind until a smooth powder.

Cut one end off the garlic head and rub lamb all over with the cut end. Then rub lamb all over on all sides with the olive oil. Mix together the lemon juice and honey and set aside. Season entire lamb leg by rubbing liberally with the spice blend. Roast at 275°F for 2½ hours. Then brush with honey and lemon juice mixture and place back in oven for 15 minutes. Top with tomato jam (recipe follows).

Tomato Jam

1 tablespoon butter	¼ cup light brown sugar
2 tablespoons ginger	1 teaspoon cumin
2 cloves chopped garlic	⅛ teaspoon cloves
¼ cup cider vinegar	¼ teaspoon cayenne
2½ pounds peeled, chopped tomatoes	¼ cup honey

Put all ingredients into small skillet or saucepan. Bring to boil, reduce heat to simmer, and let simmer for 30 minutes.

Courtesy of Chef Ryan Parrott of Local (p. 104)

Buffalo Meat Loaf

The atmosphere in Go West is what you might expect in Oklahoma. The Southwest style is abundant and so are the steaks. At Go West, Chef John McEachern serves Southwest with a flair and you'll find many ingredients native to these parts. When my husband I dined there last, Chef John recommended this meat loaf and it was an instant hit with us. You'll see why this place is beautifully elegant, yet you'll feel completely comfortable, much like this dressed-up meat loaf that is homey and wonderful.

Makes 2 six-cup meatloafs

2⅓ pounds ground buffalo meat
1⅓ pounds ground sirloin
1⅓ pounds ground beef (80/20)
5 eggs
1¾ cups panko bread crumbs
2 tablespoon cumin seed
2 tablespoons garlic, minced
3 oz. from 1 (10 oz.) can Rotel tomatoes

½ cup cilantro, chopped
½ cup Worcestershire sauce
1⅓ cup Monterey jack cheese, grated
⅓ cup Tabasco sauce
¾ cup brown sugar

Preheat oven to 350°F. Combine all ingredients in mixing bowl. Mix well on medium speed for 3–5 minutes. Lightly grease two six-cup loaf pans. Pat mixture into pans and pack down mixture. Cover with foil and bake until internal meat temperature is 175°F, around 1 hour, to 1 hour and 15 minutes. Let rest in refrigerator overnight before unmolding and slicing (very important). Slice at 1-inch thickness, plate, and reheat. Microwave until heated through on high, about 5 minutes per loaf.

Courtesy of Executive Chef John McEachern and John Wimpy,
Owner of Go West Restaurant and Saloon (p. 165)

Pecan Coffee Cake

Chef Donnie Cashion was born in Oklahoma City and spent his childhood summers in Houston, where he gained a love for cooking while spending time with his grandmother in the kitchen. After several cooking jobs in Oklahoma City, he headed to Le Cordon Bleu, Paris, and then studied and traveled in Europe for 2 years before returning to Dallas, where he had the opportunity to work for Chef Tom Colicchio at the W Hotel. Chef Cashion eventually moved back to Oklahoma and became the executive chef at Republic Gastropub, where he puts his creative modern spin on Irish pub food. A waiter suggested this dessert when I dined there one day for lunch and it instantly became my dessert of choice at Republic. I am thrilled Chef Cashion is sharing it with us for this book.

Yields one 8-inch coffee cake

- ¼ teaspoon baking soda
- ½ cup buttermilk
- 4 ounces softened butter
- 1½ cups granulated sugar
- ½ tablespoon pure vanilla extract
- ¼ teaspoon salt
- 3 eggs
- 1 tablespoon cinnamon
- ¼ cup toasted pecans

Preheat oven to 350°F. In a small bowl, combine baking soda and buttermilk and set aside. In an electric mixer, cream the butter, sugar, vanilla, and salt until light and fluffy, occasionally stopping to scrape the sides of the bowl. Next, add the eggs, a little at a time, until mixed. Add the flour and the buttermilk mixture, again stopping to scrape the sides of the mixing bowl and paddle. Mix until just combined.

Place half of the batter in a parchment-lined and buttered 8 x 8-inch cake pan and sprinkle with half of the cinnamon and half of the pecans. Then top with the remaining batter, cinnamon, and pecans.

Bake for 60 minutes in convection oven at low fan or 60 minutes in a conventional oven, or just until firm to the touch on top. Pour caramel sauce over top of coffee cake (recipe below).

Caramel Sauce

2 cups sugar
1 cup water
2 cups cream

1 teaspoon vanilla
Pinch sea salt

Bring the sugar and water to a simmer in a stainless-steel saucepan. Continue simmering, without stirring, until the sugar is amber brown. Remove from heat and add the cream slowly, whisking constantly. Be careful of the hot steam! Add vanilla and salt at end, and stir.

Courtesy of Executive Chef Donnie Cashion of Republic Gastropub (p. 43)

Mama Bennett's Coconut Cake

Chef John Bennett is a legendary world-class chef based right here in Oklahoma. Born and raised in the oilfields of Ardmore and Healdton in the 1940s, he was lured away from journalism school by cooking, and instead became a Culinary Institute of America alumnus. He was friends with and studied with the late James Beard and had a lifelong friendship with Julia Child. He has been the creative genius behind many Oklahoma restaurant kitchens and was the first culinary director/executive chef of the James Beard Awards Reception in 1991, and has presented there five times to a sold-out crowd. He hasn't lost his Oklahoma roots after traveling and tasting the world, and this cake is proof! His father, C. K. Bennett, always loved this cake the second day, when the filling had seeped into the cake, but John says it never really lasted that long! Do not refrigerate the cake as it loses its supple taste and texture.

Yields 1 cake

- 1 cup Crisco shortening
- 2 cup superfine sugar or granulated sugar put through a food processor
- 8 egg yolks (reserve whites, 6 in one dish, 2 in another)
- 1½ cups milk
- 3 teaspoons baking powder
- 1 teaspoon pure vanilla extract
- 3 cups cake flour, triple sifted and measured afterward

Preheat oven to 350°F. Cream the Crisco in mixer and gradually add the sugar until light and fluffy. Add the egg yolks, one at a time, beating well after each addition. Add ½ cup of the milk with the baking powder. Add the vanilla. Alternately add the rest of the milk with the flour, frequently scraping down sides of bowl. Mix until just incorporated and light.

Divide batter among four 9-inch cake pans that have been buttered and floured or sprayed with cooking spray and dusted with flour. You may also put in parchment cake circles that have been similarly treated.

Bake about 25 minutes until light brown and the cake springs back to the touch. Remove, cool a few minutes, then turn out.

Filling

2 of the 8 reserved egg whites
½ cup superfine sugar
6 tablespoons cake flour
2½ cups milk, heated in
    nonstick saucepan

4 tablespoons butter
2 teaspoon vanilla extract
¾ cup Angel Flake coconut

In a mixer beat the egg whites until not quite stiff; beat in the sugar then the flour.

Pour a small amount of the hot milk into this egg white, sugar, and flour paste, stirring with a whisk. Add this warmed mixture back to the milk in the saucepan and place over low heat and cook until thick. Remove and add butter, vanilla, and coconut.

While the filling is warm but not hot, assemble the cool cake dividing the filling between the three layers then topping with the fourth layer. Often I will put skewers or toothpicks to hold the cake layers together until the filling has cooled and firmed up.

Icing

6 reserved egg whites
½ teaspoon cream of tartar

1 cup superfine sugar
1 cup Angel Flake coconut

Beat the remaining egg whites in mixer with cream of tartar until soft peaks form. Add 1 cup superfine sugar, beating until incorporated. Do not overbeat or the icing will be too stiff. Ice the cake, then use Angel Flake coconut to coat top and sides Allow to set 30 minutes, then cut with a cake breaker or a large knife dipped in hot water.

Courtesy of Chef John Bennett of legendary Oklahoma fame

Appendix A: Eateries by Cuisine

American
Lucky's Restaurant, 172

Asian Fusion
Hmong Cafe, 196
KEO, 169
O Asian Fusion, 106
Te Kei's, 178
Yokozuna, 180

Austrian
Siegi's Sausage Factory, 212

Bakery
Ann's Bakery, 185
Blue Moon Bakery & Cafe, 155
Brown's Bakery, 142
Crimson N Whipped Cream, 119

Dara Marie's Gift Boutique and
    Bakery, 120
La Baguette Bistro, 86
Pancho Anaya Mexican Bakery, 203
Prairie Thunder Bakery, 145
Queenie's Plus, 175
Raspberries N Crème, 91
Sweet Cherries Sugar Art
    Bakery, 92
Sweete Memories Bakery, 93

Barbecue
Earl's Rib Palace, 108
Elmer's BBQ, 183
Head Country BBQ Restaurant, 224
Ken's Steaks & Ribs, 224
Leo's BBQ, 50
Smokin Joe's Rib Ranch, 230

Joe Momma's, 168
Sergio's Italian Bistro, 110
Stella, 139
Tucci's Cafe Italia, 178
Victoria's Pasta Shop, 113

Japanese
Fuji Japanese Cuisine & Sushi
    Bar, 164
Fusion Cafe, 102
Nhinja Sushi & Wok, 72
O Asian Fusion, 106
Pachinko Parlor, 137
Sushi Bar, The, 78
Sushi Neko, 46
Tokyo Japanese Restaurant, 80
Tokyo Pot, 231

Kolaches
Kolache Kitchen, 69

Korean
Fusion Cafe, 102
Korean Garden, 196
Seoul Garden, 229

Latin American
Cafe Antigua, 29
1492, New World Latin Cuisine,
    129
Zarates Latin Mexican Grill, 81

Lebanese Steak House
Eddy's Steakhouse, 183
Jamil's Steakhouse, 49

Mediterranean
Greek House, The, 116
Mediterranean Grill, The, 104
Nunu's Mediterranean Cafe and
    Market, 72
Shish-Kabob's, 199
Zorba's Mediterranean Cuisine, 82

Mexican
Abel's Mexican Restaurant, 56
Birrieria Diaz, 57
Elote Cafe, 162
Iguana Mexican Grill, 130
La Hacienda, 170
Pepe Delgado's, 109
Tarahumaras Mexican Cafe, 112

Southwestern
Cheever's Cafe, 32
Redrock Canyon Grill, 74

Spanish
El Pollo Chulo, 63
Bolero Spanish Grill & Tapas
　Bar, 125

Steak House
Artichoke Restaurant and Bar,
　The, 219
Boulevard Steakhouse, 58
Cardigan's Restaurant & Bar, 214
Cattlemen's Steakhouse, 115
Coach House, The, 82
Deep Fork Grill, 34
Dooley's Angus Inn, 193
Eddy's Steakhouse, 183
Go West Restaurant and
　Saloon, 165
Haunted House, The, 85
Hefner Grill, 64
Jamil's Steakhouse, 49
Junior's, 85
Ken's Steaks & Ribs, 224
Legend's Restaurant, 118

Michael's Grill, 86
Michael V's Restaurant
　& Bar, 210
Mickey Mantle's Steakhouse, 134
Molly's Landing, 225
Paseo Grill, 40
Rancher's Club, The, 228
Ranch Steakhouse, 73
Red PrimeSteak, 43
Riverside Grill, 211
Rusty Barrell Supper Club, 228
Signature Grill, 78
Smoke, On Cherry Street, 175
Waterfront Grill, 213
West, 80
White Dog Hill, 231
Wild Fork, 180

Sushi
Nhinja Sushi & Wok, 72
Sushi Bar, The, 78
Sushi Neko, 46
Sushi Place, The, 177
Tokyo Japanese Restaurant, 80
Waterfront Grill, 213
Yokozuna, 180

Sweets
Beans & Leaves, 50
Cuppies and Joe, 51
Custard Factory, 119
Green Goodies by Tiffany, 89
Kaiser's American Bistro, 131
Pinkitzel Cupcakes and Candy, 144
Sara Sara Cupcakes, 145

Tea
Beans & Leaves, 50
Inspirations Tea Room, 67
T, an Urban Teahouse, 93

Tex-Mex
El Guapo's Cantina, 162
1492, New World Latin
    Cuisine, 129

Thai
Charm Restaurant, 61
Lemongrass Thai, 69
My Thai, 173
Panang, 107
Sweet Basil Thai Cuisine, 111
Tana Thai Bistro, 79

Vegan
Matthew Kenney OKC, 37

Vegetarian
Cafe Samana, 157
Red Cup, The, 42
Matthew Kenney OKC, 37
Queen of Sheba, 73

Vietnamese
Lee's Sandwiches, 36
Pho Da Cao, 198
Pho Lien Hoa, 40
Saigon Baguette, 46
Viet Huong, 201

Wine Bar
Cellar at Main Street Wine Depot,
    The, 222
Kamp's 1910 Cafe & The
    Vineyard, 132
Mantel Wine Bar & Bistro,
    The, 134
Michelangelo's Coffee and Wine
    Bar, 106
Panevino Wine & Tapas Bar, 226
Sonoma Bistro & Wine Bar, 176

Appendix B: Dishes, Specialties & Specialty Food

Marshall Brewing Company, 236
Mustang Brewing Company, 237
Redbud Brewing Company, 238

Coffee, Tea & Wine
Beans & Leaves, 50
Beatnix Cafe, The, 141
Blue Bean Coffee, 119
Cafe Cubana, 186
Cafe Topeca Coffee Shop, 186
Cellar at Main Street Wine Depot,
    The, 222
Coffee House on Cherry Street, 188
Coffee Slingers, 142
Cuppies & Joe, 51
Gray Owl Coffee, 120
Inspirations Tea Room, 67
Kamp's 1910 Cafe & The
    Vineyard, 132
Mantel Wine Bar & Bistro, The, 134
Mecca Coffee, 189
Michelangelo's Coffee and Wine
    Bar, 106
Panevino Wine & Tapas Bar, 226
Shades of Brown Coffee & Art, 191
Sonoma Bistro & Wine Bar, 176
T, an Urban Teahouse, 93
Vintage Timeless Coffee, 94

Cooking Classes
Cooking Girl, 94
Francis Tuttle School of Culinary
    Arts, 95
Kam's Kookery and Guilford
    Gardens, 97
Matthew Kenney Academy, 53
Table One, 146

Deli
Beatnix Cafe, The, 141
Brown Bag Deli, 59
Dilly Deli, 160
Earth Natural Cafe & Deli,
    The, 100
Lambrusco'z to Go, 189
Stuffed Olive, The, 111
Two Olives Cafe, 113

Dim Sum
Guang Zhou Dim Sum, 195

Ethnic Grocers
Ferria Latina Market, 89
Lovera's Famous Italian
    Market, 233
Spices of India Market, 92
Super Cao Nguyen Asian Market, 52

Index